To: The Ambitious
From: The Experienced
26 LETTERS ON LEADERSHIP

A. JORDAN FISCHETTE

To: The Ambitious
From: The Experienced
26 Letters on Leadership

First Edition
Published by Paddle Boat Printing

For bulk sales please contact the publisher.

Concept by A. Jordan Fischette
Editor-in chief: Mary Slifer
Interior Design by Kristen Voll

Paddle Boat Printing
www.paddleboatprinting.com

ISBN-13: 978-1548726850
ISBN-10: 1548726850

Library of Congress Control Number: 2017916601

Proudly Printed in the United States of America

DEDICATION

To my parents, the first leaders I ever learned from.

ACKNOWLEDGEMENTS

This book couldn’t be possible without the support of my family, friends and colleagues. Thank you for the constant support, the daily wake up calls, and the commitment to my growth.

A very special thank you to all of the contributors who helped to make this book a reality. I, literally, couldn’t have made this dream a reality without you! I will forever be indebted to each of you. Note: this book is not intended to be used as an eternal reminder of favors owed. ☺

Most importantly, the biggest thank you goes to my right-hand woman, Kristen. The 5 am wake-up calls, midnight brainstorm sessions and constant revisions would've driven most people to the brink, I like to pretend they didn't do that to you! I am grateful for your friendship and lucky to have you on my team.

FOREWORD

The Fitness Expert

Leadership has always come naturally to me: not easily, but naturally. No doubt it has been my innate aversion to being told what to do myself that fueled my entrepreneurial spirit throughout life. At the age of 13, I had a babysitting and neighborhood home-cleaning business. At 20, I was working my way through college as a shift manager at Moe's Southwest Grill, a position I scored after just one month. From the age of 22, I've essentially started and run my own businesses, everything from marketing myself as an actress, to starting Broadway Babysitters (a babysitting agency in NYC), to what I do now as a certified personal trainer. Currently, I own a personal training studio and have a thriving presence, nationally, online and in print, as a published fitness expert. I continue to be very successful as a business owner and it absolutely has everything to do with the leadership skills I've learned along the way. My success as a fitness leader has been dependent on being able to effectively equip clients with the right skills to be able to take control over their own lives and attain a higher quality of life. I know that when one lives more healthfully, it bleeds over into every other aspect of work life and relationships. I'll say it again because there are few more important truths. When my clients are successful at leading healthy lives, they are far more successful at work and in relationships. Here are five of the most important lessons I lead clients to master that help them to stop only talking about reaching fitness goals and be successful and do it!

Take Control Back

Sounds like a no brainer tip, right? Human beings have an innate desire to be in control and make their own decisions. Studies on human behavior in the workplace have shown that individual employees and work teams are more productive, more creative, more successful and enjoy their jobs more deeply when their leaders provide an environment that fosters and encourages taking more control over projects. The following example sheds light on how we can apply this to our personal life- specifically our health goals. When you wake up one day and you say to yourself, "Where in the world did this extra 30lbs come from and why do I feel so exhausted all the time?" The short answer is that you lost control. You stopped being in control of your own health. No one did that but you and only you can take that control back. It starts with a decision. Make the decision that YOU are in control over YOU: nobody or nothing else. When you empower yourself by mentally taking this control back, you have made the first step in the right direction and you are on your way to becoming the best version of yourself.

Break It Down

You've made the decision to take control, so now it's time to set some health goals. Write down your goals because it gives them power; share them with others because it gives you accountability. But here's the trick to goal setting because goals can be overwhelming to tackle unless we break big goals into smaller, more achievable goals. Create a flow chart from your big goals and begin by tackling the smaller goals first. For example, if your goal is to lose 30lbs by the end of the year, you'll need to make some lifestyle changes. Write each one of these lifestyle changes you need to make and start implementing them ONE by ONE. Master one before you move on to the next goal. Again, we're trying to eliminate the "overwhelming" factor that often causes failure. When you can break your goals down to smaller more achievable goals that you can master one at a time, you'll have a greater sense of accomplishment as you move from one small goal to another. Changing your lifestyle habits is a marathon, it's not a sprint. You didn't pack on 30lbs over night; you won't lose it overnight.

Take It Day By Day

Defeat is part of the road to success! It will happen that you will have days that are total washes, days you didn't meet any of your small goals. It may even happen that you go a whole week without meeting any of your goals. Remember that success does not follow a linear upward path. All the Greats' success stories have been marked with failure along the way. We tend to assume successful people had it easy, that they have it all together and never struggled to achieve their greatness. That assumption couldn't be farther from the truth. All great stories are marked by failures. So take your goals day by day, putting yesterday completely behind you. It is neither here nor there. Don't let the failures impede your ultimate progress. Remember that it's all a part of the journey. Trust the process! It is only important that the sum of your successes be greater than the sum of your failures.

Find Some Cheerleaders

You can't do this alone, period. Accountability and having a team behind you might be the greatest factor in achieving your goals. You've got to get your friends and family on board with this lifestyle change or you won't make it. A support system is vital. If your family won't get on board, turn to friends. If your friends aren't supportive, get new ones! Hire a trainer. Join a social media support group. You need people to hold you accountable, cheer you on, and do it with you. It takes your initiative to create this support network for yourself. You'll oftentimes have to go out of your way to put this in place, but we are more successful when we know we are not in this alone. Don't let momentum fizzle out because you have no one to answer to.

Be the Inspiration

Make yourself an authority on eating healthier and being more fit. You must realize that you don't have to have it perfectly together to be the inspiration for others. Besides, none of us have it all together. Not even we fitness pros! When you give yourself that responsibility, you create pressure on yourself to keep moving forward. People are looking to you for guidance; they depend on you. Share your struggles along with your successes. It's rewarding to help others. I truly know that is what we are all meant to do on this earth. Sharing your journey always helps somebody, whether you are aware of it or not.

Overall, these five most important lessons will help you master a healthier lifestyle, stay in control of your destiny, and create healthier habits. It's hard at first, no doubt. But by taking it day by day, choice by choice, you will succeed in leading an inspiring life that others, but most importantly you, will be grateful forever!

***

Hannah Davis, certified strength and conditioning specialist (CSCS), will always be a coastal Carolinian at heart. Born and raised in North Carolina, Hannah first fell in love with weight training in high school when she was just 17. She was a cheerleader, ran cross-country, and played soccer - but nothing fascinated her quite as much as weight training. She graduated from UNC-Greensboro with a degree in drama and left to chase her acting dreams in New York City.

After a couple daytime drama TV appearances and a few stage gigs, she started working at a talent agency. Trapped behind a desk and the politics of the industry, Hannah found herself suffering from "real world" anxiety that was no longer being managed by daily trips to the gym – her meditative time. A year into working with the agency, she had a eureka moment when she decided she wanted to be doing something with her life that would improve someone else's quality of life. There was one thing she knew she was really good at - understanding the roles of exercise and nutrition in achieving complete wellness. She left her desk job and enrolled in the Academy of Personal Training in NYC, where she graduated at the top of her class.

Hannah's many certifications enable her to work with clients who are training for weight loss, muscle hypertrophy, corrective exercise, specific sport, and pre/post natal. She has worked with children, athletes, young professionals and the elderly. She is experienced with addressing a variety of limitations that clients may have. Her background in nutrition also adds a strong component to creating a more complete training program.

Hannah served as the fitness expert on the advisory board for Cosmopolitan Magazine and has contributed to publications and books including Women's Health Magazine, Cosmopolitan, SELF, Fitness Magazine, Health Magazine, Yahoo Health and the Rodale-published book, Shape Up Shortcuts to name a few. She has appeared on NYC's Fox 5 and NY 1.

Currently, Hannah lives in Cleveland, TN where she trains privately in her studio location in downtown Cleveland and hosts her own fitness show on WTNB.

INTRODUCTION

The Author

Oftentimes I find myself posing a question to my friends, "do you ever think about the different roles we play in life?" The typical initial response is a "what the heck are you talking about?" Once I explain what I mean it always turns into an interesting conversation.

You see, I have this belief that everyone has different versions of themselves. This doesn't make us disingenuous; in fact, it might be the most human part of us. Now let me clarify. I don't mean we're a grammar school teacher by day and vigilante by night. What I mean is that we aren't the same to our boss as we are to our significant other, or to our parents, or to our sibling, and the list goes on.

When I graduated college, I started working for a Division I fraternity as a consultant. It was this job that got me thinking not only about the roles we play but their link to leadership. When I visited a chapter for work, I was viewed as the subject matter expert. They may not have always liked what I had to say but they knew that I was there to help, and that I had been trained to assist them.

When I returned to the office, I was the youngest consultant, the new guy. I wasn't treated as though I was inferior but I would hold my tongue until others spoke (Bobby, if you're reading this stop laughing.) It was a sort of a self-imposed restriction. Cultural norms told me that I should listen to what the older guys had to say. I needed to earn my stripes, or so I told myself.

Then the professional conferences started. I'd go from being the head honcho on a campus, to the new guy in the office, to the... well nothing at the conference. They had a first timer track. They gave us a ribbon on our nametags that said "First Timer." I remember telling one of my friends "why don't they just put a sign on our backs that say 'KICK ME'?" I honestly don't think anyone was outright cruel to me or intentionally demeaning at the conference but there was a lot of patronizing and "that's cute" attitudes thrown my way. You know, when you speak and someone looks at you with... that look. They might not open their mouths, but you distinctly hear them say "you didn't just say that, right?"

Finally, that year, I went home for Christmas. As the baby of the family, my role changed yet again. I may not be the smartest, that goes to Matt, and I am certainly not the prettiest, looking at you Jess, but I had my own special place. I like to think of my role as the favorite but they'd probably dispute that.

I think there are three major facets of leadership that living through these roles taught me:

1. Everyone has inherent leadership abilities.
2. Leadership is exhibited in more ways than I ever imagined.
3. Cultural norms dictate our perceptions and actions more than we realize.

As an avid learner and someone who just consumes information about topics I find fascinating, I found myself, for lack of a less embarrassing term, obsessed with leadership. I decided to go to graduate school and focus on learning more about leadership.

Now, there will certainly be some who disagree with

what I'm about to say, but you can just buy their book later to know their thoughts!

There are researchers and there are practitioners. In my career, I am surrounded by both. It took me a while to see the distinction and understand why it exists, but now that I am aware of it, it is something I think about often.

The easiest way to explain it is like this. Think of Chemistry class. There's a class and a lab, right? In class you permutate, calculate, read, study, test, theorize and more. Those are researchers. In lab you fill a balloon with hydrogen, put a match near it and enjoy the show! Those are practitioners.

I find that I am much more of a natural practitioner than I am researcher. Don't get me wrong - I love research but I don't enjoy the process of conducting it. Rather, I enjoy taking their findings and applying them to the real world. I want to see how real-life people and situations react to leadership versus studying an intentional control group.

Okay... I want to get this squared away upfront. Here's what this book is and is not:

- It is not an extensively researched, doctoral thesis level publication.
- It is a conversational piece.
- It is the spark that can ignite your creativity.
- It is an authentic glimpse into the way real people use actual leadership in their everyday lives.

When I came up with the idea for this book I thought about asking friends to tell me what they've learned about leadership from their lives. That seemed too basic and overdone for my taste. As I've told you already, I am fascinated by the roles we play in life, so I decided to write a book in a similar way. I asked them to write through the lens of a specific persona. For most, that persona is their career.

Nearly everyone was hesitant. I don't think I've ever had so many people tell me they're not writers. I assured them that the goal was not to have countless stories written by English professors. What I wanted was authentic stories. Stories from the heart. Stories that others could relate to.

My instruction was essentially this, "when someone reads your story it should be as though they're sitting next to you. Write as though you're having a conversation. Tell your story in YOUR voice." They took my advice and the letters came.

I expected to get some great stories I could compile and add to this book. I expected to laugh a little and maybe shed a tear. I expected to have to hunt people down for their submissions, but what I got was so much more. I learned about taking initiative from a young Fashionista in the heart of New York City. I discovered what discipline really means from a Marine. I learned how to listen, I mean, really listen, from a Cosmetologist.

What does the Engineer do onboard when a crisis occurs at sea? How do you control your excitement when you're asked to be a Coordinator for the Super Bowl when you're a total sports fanatic? What do you do when your boss asks you to make a magazine and the closest thing you have to experience is shuffling through a Vogue at your last hair appointment?

You'll find answers to all of those questions and I hope, much more.

Ready? Let's get started.

Contents

The Google Engineer

If I do something wrong, the entire internet goes down. Okay, perhaps that is a bit of an exaggeration. Nevertheless, that is how it feels being a software engineer who works on Google Pub/Sub, a part of the company's infrastructure relied upon by nearly all of Google's products. While I had worked on important pieces of software infrastructure in prior jobs, nothing fully prepared me for the challenges of working on a system as large in scale as Google Pub/Sub.

When I started at Google, I was tasked with maintaining the newest part of Pub/Sub: a program that stores the state of the clients that are connected to the system. This new program was replacing some older programs that could no longer handle the massive amount of data we needed to access quickly. The task seemed overwhelming at the beginning for many different reasons. First of all, I knew how important the system was. If it failed, the effects could be catastrophic for Pub/Sub. Secondly, I had an unbelievable amount to learn about the Pub/Sub system, Google's extensive set of tools and libraries I would build on top of, and--most fundamentally--the programming language I was going to use, which I had not touched in six years. Finally, I put myself under some self-imposed pressure to do a good job in the eyes of my manager and my technical lead.

My manager was a friend of mine who I had known for seven years, having met him at my first job. He was someone whose judgement I trusted completely. He was the driving force who made Google Pub/Sub what it is today. My technical lead, the person who shapes the building blocks that make up a system and guide its development, was someone I knew from my days as a graduate student. He was a very smart person for whom I had overseen a research project while he was an undergrad.

That would sound like the dream scenario: working for talented people who already knew me! While that made it easier to adjust to a new job, it also meant that the expectations were higher. They knew my work and knew what I had done in the past, so they figured I would do the same at Google.

My technical lead oversaw my first project and set me up for success, a key quality in the best leaders I have worked with. The program I was to work on was already about 70% complete. My technical lead started me on a very small piece of the system: adding support so that when one machine running the program failed, the program running on another machine could take over without any interruptions. The addition required only a small amount of well-defined code, limiting the number of new things I had to learn to complete my task. It allowed me to focus on learning only a small part of the system at once. Over time, my projects would encompass more of the system.

While working on my first project, there were a lot of things I didn't know and I needed to find answers. With any large tech company, there are a lot of pieces that others have built that engineers try to reuse whenever possible: there is no reason to rewrite that which already exists. Sometimes finding those pieces can be difficult if you don't know exactly what to search for. When I couldn't find answers, I would need to ask my technical lead for more information.

Figuring out what questions to ask and when to ask them can be a daunting task in and of itself. People often say "there are no stupid questions." In many ways, that is true. However, that adage does not mean "ask any question anytime without trying to find the answer first." I didn't want to ask questions without doing my own research. If I asked my technical lead too many simple questions, he might think I'm not taking the time to investigate and solve problems on my own, an important part of my job description. If I wait too long to ask questions, I could get stuck and not make forward progress on my project.

In order to make sure I did ask good questions, I looked at many existing examples of code that accomplished tasks similar to my goal. Additionally, my technical lead had pointed out several tutorials that gave good walkthroughs on the libraries I would need to use. I studied those extensively, taking care to do all of the exercises they provided so I could become more familiar with the tools I knew I'd be using from that point forward. As I started implementing the code for my first project, I would refer back to the examples and library tutorials before I'd ask my technical lead any questions; I didn't want to ask questions that were answered in the materials he provided me with! My technical lead would certainly not have minded answering them, but I didn't think it would reflect well on me. Even with all of the information I had access to, I still had some questions. Sometimes they would be questions about how to use particular functions I needed to call. In those cases, I would tell my technical lead what I did know and ask him very specific questions. Other times they were questions where I wasn't sure of the best approach to take. I would present a couple of options and ask for his advice. After getting answers to my questions and following his suggestions, I was ready to add my first bits of code to the extensive Google codebase.

One of the most dreaded times for a new software engineer at a company is the first code review. Whenever one is about to submit changes to a program--changes that will inevitable be released for use by the entire world--the changes are first reviewed by at least one other engineer. It is a rite of passage for an engineer to submit that first set of changes. In my case, my first code review was performed by my technical lead. How much was he going to hate the code I wrote? Was he going to find very obvious bugs that I missed? What if I did everything wrong?

My first code review contained 25 comments. In case you are wondering, 25 is a large number of comments relative to the size of the changes I was making, but that is not unusual for one's first code review. Thankfully, my technical lead was the kind of person who was very constructive in his comments. There were places he could have said, "You called the wrong function here." Instead, he would say "Should you be calling a different function here? Can you add a test case?" The subtle difference in tone in those two comments conveys the same message very differently. The first one says, "You are wrong and you need to fix this." The second says "Check and see if you are wrong and in either case, verify the answer." Of course, I was wrong, but the comment my technical lead sent empowered me to figure that out for myself.

That first code review took a couple of days of going back and forth. My technical lead would make more suggestions as I made changes and I would make more changes. The comments continued to be constructive and made me feel like I was learning more with each one. Every time, I took his comments seriously. Sometimes, he would make small stylistic recommendations that I didn't necessarily agree with, but didn't have a strong enough opinion to reject, so I would just make the changes. I find it is very important to pick one's battles. Eventually, I got the coveted "LGTM," or "looks good to me," meaning I had permission to integrate my changes with the rest of Google Pub/Sub.

That was the first of many code changes I have made. Since then, I have taken ownership of several pieces of our Pub/Sub infrastructure. Now, I don't just implement small changes, I am given large-scale problems to solve from beginning to end. I have to start with a design document that outlines the problem, propose a solution, and compare it to other possible solutions. I have also made a point of asking for more responsibilities when I can, including an effort to improve our documentation. Taking the initiative in identifying and solving problems allows me to learn more about our system in order to become more invaluable.

From my first project at Google to the diverse work I do today, I learned that being successful in a new environment has two important parts: being set up for success by good leaders and setting yourself up to follow through. A good leader assumes from the beginning that you are very good at what you do and gives you the opportunity to shine. I have been fortunate enough to work for several people with this mentality. When the person you are working for has confidence in you, it is easier to have confidence in yourself, even when starting on a project that is completely new and overwhelming to you.

However, a good leader setting you up for success does not guarantee you will be successful. Ultimately, the power is in your own hands. You have to research on your own, ask good questions, learn from feedback, and push yourself to take on more challenging work. Whether a leader trusts you from the beginning or expects you to earn it over time, you need to do the work that ultimately shows that you deserve that trust.

***

Kamal Aboul-Hosn is a software engineer at Google on the Cloud Pub/Sub team. Before coming to

Google, he spent time at a diverse set of companies, including Bloomberg, Meridian, and Square. He has worked on all levels of the development stack, from front-end applications on the web, Android, and iOS platforms to integral pieces of infrastructure in critical systems. Kamal earned his Ph.D. from Cornell University. In his spare time, he plays drums in the band Not All Heroes and enjoys photography.

The Chief Marketing Officer

I had been in a marketing leader role pretty comfortably for the last two years, and then my boss, the CEO, had his next big idea, which it was my job to implement.

"Publish a magazine," he says. My first thought was that he had lost his mind. What did we know about producing a magazine? But he was serious. He set his expectations and gave me a deadline. It was my job to execute. Easy enough, right? Not for this marketing leader, who had never before in her life published anything close to a print magazine similar to Inc., or Fortune, the two magazines my boss so admired. Write a few blogs? Sure, no problem. An e-book? Again, not a problem. But a full blown, print magazine that would be distributed to our list of subscribers (which, by the way, I also needed to build in parallel to producing the magazine), both in print and digital formats? Never.

The task seemed overwhelming. Where should I even start? I began where I always do with something new - research. I hopped online and googled to learn more. It immediately became apparent that I would need to make some connections in the world of publishing. I decided to do what I do best in situations of the unknown – "fast follow" someone I admire, some other company that does a great job at what I'm trying to accomplish. So I picked up the latest edition of Inc. magazine and read through a few of the articles. I found an author that I really liked, and decided, what the heck, it won't hurt to contact her. And it was a good thing I did! Not only did she agree to write our feature article, and several of the smaller ones, but she also had a large network of writer friends. She was able to help me source every single article quickly, and all would be written by professional writers, the same writers who wrote for the exact magazines I was trying to emulate.

So, my first problem was solved, but there were several more to tackle. Once I had the written articles, then what? They had to be laid out into some sort of magazine format with great visuals and great photography. I'm not a graphic artist. Nor did I have one on my staff. What was I to do? Again, it was all about who you know. I scoured my network. Who did I know in the graphic design business? And if they weren't able to help, who did they know? With a little luck, and a little tenacity, I was able to locate a friend of a friend who was willing to take on our inaugural magazine as a free-lance project (in addition to his day job, and for probably a lot less than he was used to. (Thank goodness for small favors!)

I now had the content, and the design, but I was missing a key ingredient: an audience. This was one area that I knew my way around. What I needed was a marketing campaign. I knew our target audience – sales and marketing leaders in mid to large B2B companies. I knew what I wanted them to do – subscribe to our magazine. I knew what channels to use – email, phone and social media. I designed and launched a campaign immediately. And the response was great. We rounded up a few thousand subscribers right off the bat. Not bad for a small company trying to publish its first print magazine for sales and marketing leaders.

The final pieces were production and distribution. How the heck was I actually going to get the magazine printed and shipped out to our newly acquired audience? Google was once again my friend. I began searching for print shops. I also used some of my co-workers expertise. Turns out he was a former sales rep for a print company, and I was able to take advantage of his knowledge. He helped me know what questions to ask, what specs to ask for and so on.

We were off to the races. The content was written by professional, top of the line writers. The magazine lay-out was being handled by a great freelance designer who worked quickly and for the right price. And I had a major print shop that had agreed to print the copies we needed, and drop them in the mail for our audience. It was a long road, but I could finally see the light at the end of the tunnel.

Now, this isn't to say there weren't bumps along the way. My CEO hated the first layout we presented to him, so it was back to the drawing board. We had a photographer flake out on us the last minute, and I nearly killed myself trying to find a replacement. The first print proof sent to me was also terrible, absolutely terrible – wrong paper, binding, etc. But they were all mistakes we were able to overcome. And the best part? We were able to overcome them in time to hit the deadline imposed by my CEO. We were able to make a big "reveal" at our annual company kick-off meeting. Nothing feels better than being recognized in front of your peers for a job well done.

So, what did I learn along the way? Quite a few things. First, as a leader you must learn to be comfortable being uncomfortable. Learning to produce a magazine made me extremely uncomfortable at first. Many other marketing executives may have shied away from the challenge and instead convinced their CEO to do something "safer." I didn't. I jumped in feet first. Now, a year and a half later, we are a magazine producing machine and produce an issue every single quarter. And if I don't say myself, they continue to get better and better each time.

The second big lesson is to always be acquiring new capabilities. Why? First, it makes you more marketable as a leader. Who doesn't want to work with someone who is constantly learning new skills? And second, and even more important, it makes the job more enjoyable. The challenges I face and overcome, and the skills I acquire along the way are addicting. It makes me want to work harder, to see just how far I can push myself.

***

For more than a decade, Christina has been a marketing leader. She began her career with a leading sales and marketing consultancy, creating and implementing innovating strategies. Her goal was to ensure each client met their annual revenue goals. Christina is considered a trailblazer in the marketing industry because the amount of high profile organizations she has worked with to regain control and success of their marketing initiatives. Her work has impacted companies and consumers world-wide.

Christina currently serves as the Director of Marketing for a computer software company. She lives in Zionsville, IN with her two kids, Brynn and Seth. She is a die-hard fan of the Indianapolis Colts and an avid runner.

The Dentist

"She's crazy" my assistant warned me. I sighed heavily and made my way to the operatory, dreading what kind of lunacy may be waiting for me this time.

More often than not, when a new patient enters the office, my assistant will give me some back story on the patient before I meet him or her. "They haven't seen a dentist in over 10 years" is a common warning. "He's handsome!" is the second most common, as my staff has made finding a man for my rapidly drying out ovaries their own personal Mission Impossible. This is followed, of course, by the ever so common "they're crazy."

As I begrudgingly walked to my operatory, I was greeted by a woman well in her 90s. For this story, we'll call her Ruth (not her real name). Ruth was missing quite a few teeth, had several cavities, and an endless amount of questions for me. As many people her age do, she repeated herself quite a bit during our discourse. We sat for over an hour while my assistant glared at me in a murderous rage listening to me repeat the same treatment plan over and over again. The patient finally seemed happy and satisfied enough to leave, only to return 3 more times that week with the same questions.

I wish I could say that I wasn't annoyed that I had to spend so much time repeating myself over and over. At heart, I'm a classic Type A personality who likes to plan things once, implement them once, and get immediate and perfect results. However, with Ruth, it was clear this was not going to happen. Time and time again, I swallowed my nature and repeated myself. However, the more time I spent with Ruth, the more I learned from her. The more patience I showed her, the more patience my staff had for her. Soon, we all looked forward to our extra long appointments with Ruth.

That's when I realized that whenever I see a patient, I am silently leading by example in small ways every day. Dentistry is one of those professions you don't realize is physically and mentally taxing until you start working. No matter how much you love this career, it can be difficult to maintain a positive outlook after hearing "I hate you" from a near stranger fifty seven times a day. After my experience with Ruth, it was apparent that every time I go into a situation with a preconceived notion or a bad attitude, I am silently and unknowingly giving my staff permission to do the same.

I started to focus on putting my preconceived notions aside and truly listen to what my patients were saying. "I hate the dentist" often means "the last person I trusted with my oral health let me down." Someone who comes in angry and screaming often feels like their problems are not being listened to and addressed. Someone who does not want to invest in their health often hasn't been taught the value of their bodies.

When we think of having leadership abilities, usually we think of outward signs such as being confident, being able to handle difficult situations, and the ability to effectively delegate tasks. What's often taken for granted are the small things, such as the ability to empathize with people, to constantly keep learning, and to accurately listen to someone. Taking the extra time to listen to what someone means is what makes the difference between someone simply being in a leadership position and someone leading with integrity.

Once I started implementing this mindset with my patients, I saw it spill over to my staff in many ways. They still warn me when someone is acting crazy, but now they sit and watch the craziness (usually) melt away to reveal a human being who's just trying to make their voice heard. I also started listening to my staff more. Overhearing, "I didn't want to come in today" often means "I'm feeling overworked and underappreciated." A dental practice works as a cohesive unit. No matter what role one has within the office, he or she is vital to the success of the practice. Thanks to Ruth, I learned that in order to effectively lead my office, I must take the time to remind my staff often of how vital they are to my success.

Being open to learning experiences and taking

time to let my staff know they are appreciated has made a world of difference in office morale. I believe that the most important part of being an effective leader is to always be open to new learning experiences. New experiences have the power to change your outlook and see things in ways you never have before. No matter what level of education or job title someone has, he or she should never stop learning. Lessons come to you in a variety of different ways, whether it be a personal experience, a special course to obtain a new skill, or an elderly patient with a wealth of wisdom to pass on.

***

Anna Pietrantoni, DDS is a dentist in the Greater Boston area. She believes that a healthy mouth leads to excellent overall health. She is passionate about oral health education and makes a point to volunteer at many public health seminars, raising awareness to the link between oral health and overall health, and increasing accessibility to dental care. In addition to teeth, Anna loves her two calico cats, Persephone and Demeter, cooking healthy meals that taste like fat kid food, and occasionally having wine and sushi in a bubble bath.

The Event Mogul

With a heaviness in my head, I open my eyes to a pitch-black room with nothing but a tiny crease letting in the sunshine. Right! I'm in an enormous New Orleans convention hotel with more rooms and elevators than I've ever seen at this point in my life. Pure excitement has now taken over my entire body. This is my first tradeshow as the lead for my organization's exhibit, consisting of 12 people. Everything I have done in my career has led up to this moment. I jump out of bed and remember the two signature NOLA drinks I had the night before with a client. You know, the sugary red drink in the extra-large glass! Now on auto pilot, I get the coffee maker going, and my excitement has fully taken over my potential headache.

Once on the tradeshow floor I communicate with

my booth partners letting them know I've got everything covered and to please just show up in 3 hours and "look pretty." The hotel staff is running around delivering boxes. My boxes have not arrived, but I'm not worried. I'm still astounded by the amount of money organizations pay to pack, ship and deliver $1.50 giveaway items. However, they are absolutely necessary in the tradeshow world. I unpack a few things I brought along and call the decorator. Looking around and seeing the start of the other booths around me, I realize, our booth is going to be amazing!

A bellman comes over to greet me, and introduces himself.

"Hi I'm Nate," he says. Nate kindly informs me my boxes are going to be late and won't arrive until the second day of the event. I'm now thinking this hotel is not only the largest hotel I've ever seen, but also the smartest, as they have just sent their attractive, fresh out of college bellman to deliver me the bad news. Typically, my inner drama queen would have kicked in by now, but based on the look on his face, I knew there was nothing he could do about it. He apologizes, gives me the business center's extension, and walks away. I'm totally screwed! What are my booth partners going to think of me? Ugh, my "potential headache" from last night's spiked syrup might be creeping in!

Months before this tradeshow, my immediate boss gave me free rein for booth theme and set-up. However, since I was new to the organization, it was important to impress my co-workers/booth partners and make sure this was as memorable of an event for them as I only dreamt it would be for me. Collaborating would be our bonding moment and a way to get to know everyone as a team!

While planning for this tradeshow, we held a meeting in our office's boardroom high above the city overlooking Tampa Bay. After an exchange of many ideas, we finally decided to go with a traditional look from our city. Anytime I'm in this particular boardroom, I walk in with a sense of confidence, knowing as a team, we always walk out with true solutions and decisions. It could be the large leather back chairs and the floor to ceiling windows with views of cruise ships, or it might be the coffee and snacks, but our ideas come together brilliantly. The team decided on a city theme with flamenco dancers and a cigar roller. This theme would surely showcase the energy and synergy this team has exuded for years. Although listening and incorporating many ideas did make things challenging at times, overall we did apply most ideas, including costumes, and the planning process was successful.

Thankfully most of our team shows up to the tradeshow dressed in the exact outfits we shopped for months prior. The décor was coming along nicely. I take a deep breath hoping the bad news of the missing boxes with client giveaways does not cause outright panic amongst the team and glance around again. Yep, we have the best booth, in the best location (next to the hors d'oeuvres) and the team members present look amazing in their flamenco costumes.

As I reach for the phone to contact the agency I hired to find a cigar roller, I see a Hawaiian man in a Tommy Bahama shirt and a taller woman with fluffy hair, cut-off shorts and a crop top coming our way. The man was pulling a cart, and I quickly realize they are walking towards me. The man and woman both introduce themselves as our hired cigar roller and his interpreter. Although the man does not speak English, he has a warm smile and laughs a lot, so I know he will be a great addition to our exhibit. As I direct them to their set-up location, I take another glance at the woman. Her stomach is bare, with no apparent workout regimen and hot pink undergarments are visible as she walks away. Her self-confidence is admirable, but her unprofessional attire does not go over well with our team. Luckily, she was just there to assist with set up.

Fifteen minutes before the exhibit hall opens, I quickly do a headcount. We are clearly missing one person from our team, Rhonda. She was not known for being soft spoken, so I'm still shocked I didn't notice her absence. I gave her a call & text with no answer. As I start asking around, I'm getting these guilty looks from everyone. With no surprise, I find out the majority of the team ended up on Bourbon Street, but by the sounds of it, Rhonda might have had a few more NOLA drinks than the rest. There were tales of a leprechaun, a stage and a hula-hoop! I think to myself, "well, only one down, not bad for New Orleans!" and move on to prep the team.

The show is about to start. As I walk into the back of the exhibit hall, I see Nate, the bellman, lugging both of our boxes behind him. Phew- the partners have not even noticed these boxes missing! He smiled and said he would drop them off at the booth and I gladly handed him a $20 bill. I continued to walk behind the exhibit hall to find a quiet place. I took a deep breath and told myself, this is it. All of your planning and hard work will finally find you. Now, all I needed to do was to dig in deep inside and find charisma that once came so naturally, and turn it on!

I see the doors opening and the clients coming in the exhibit hall, and trotting behind, is Rhonda. Her eyes looked a bit tired, but the rest of her looked like she could pull this off. I thought to myself, success; everyone is here! Then, I mused, "how many people miss their meetings here after enjoying this city's charms."

My first client to visit was, Michelle, my client from the night before. She definitely surprised me with her personality. Typically an overall quiet woman, she really opened up while walking around Bourbon Street. She even taught me few clogging moves, a secret talent she shared with me. We laughed almost the entire evening and still managed to discuss her future events. It's such a pleasure when clients have the potential to become friends. I introduced Michelle to our team. Rhonda started chatting her up about her time in New Orleans and the different areas they have both already experienced. I start walking up to the cigar table to grab Michelle a cigar, and there she was- the cigar roller's interpreter; showing off her bellybutton and hot pink undergarments while attempting to have conversations with the now four clients in front of her. I didn't know what to do. She was hired through a third party so I wasn't sure of protocol. I thought to myself, do I call the agency?

Quickly, I turn around to Bethany, one of my other partners, and say, "do you see that, this is awful?" Right there, I didn't know it, but I was about to learn a lesson. Bethany looks at me with authority and says, "This is your show, do something about it." She said it so matter of fact, it almost stung, making me feel like I had failed, but I had not failed. I still had time to fix this situation. I pulled the interpreter aside and asked her to leave until the show was over. Problem fixed!

My first lesson from this event came from my immediate boss. He gave me complete creative freedom throughout the entire planning process to make this a great exhibit. With that, I knew he had confidence in me and I didn't want to disappoint him. He also made sure to always be available for guidance and support along the way if needed. In my personal experience and watching him with my other co-workers, this has been the most successful leadership endeavor I have experienced thus far.

The second lesson was from my friend and exhibit partner, Bethany. I had owned everything about the project and almost allowed a disaster to continue with the cigar roller's interpreter. When taking on a task or a project, getting your team to collaborate and be on the same page is imperative, but owning any challenges and executing solutions is your job: no one else's.

My first tradeshow with my organization was tremendously successful and we ended up on the cover of an industry publication. The lessons I learned from this show I've taken with me to every event and project over the last five years.

*names and some details have been changed to protect identities

***

Brittany represents the city of Tampa's hotels and

venues by coordinating city bids for groups of all sizes including city-wide events. She was born and raised in Tampa, FL and started working in the hotel industry as a Concierge at the age of 17. Brittany graduated with a Bachelor's degree in Interdisciplinary Social Sciences from the University of South Florida. During her studies, she attended a study abroad program at University or Cambridge in the U.K. focusing on British Literature. When Brittany is not selling the beautiful city of Tampa, she is spending time with her husband & two children Callen and Ellie.

Brittany is the National Sales Manager at Visit Tampa Bay; Hillsborough County's Convention and Visitors Bureau.

The Higher Ed Professional

You need to pay your dues. You must start at the bottom and work your way up the ladder. Both are common phrases we hear all the time about the workplace, but don't really think apply to us until we are fresh out of college and struggling to find that "perfect" job we think we are now qualified for. These days, having a bachelor's degree (and in my case a master's degree) is still often not enough to secure a job at the level that you'd expect after spending several years in school. I have found this to be especially true in the field I work in: Higher Education. In my experience, networking and accruing relevant work experience to establish a leadership presence are equally as important as education level in working toward your dream job. This is my story, a story of discovering my "brand" of leadership and learning that every experience is valuable, even if it's not what you imagined you'd be doing. What I found in my journey is that to establish this brand, I needed to put the needs and goals of my department before my own desires. This is how I came to value and embody aspects of servant leadership.

During the second half of my last semester of graduate school to obtain my M.Ed. in Higher Education, I began applying for my first "grown-up" job. Up until that point, every job I've had was part-time while I was going to school, including my graduate assistant position at that time. I applied for dozens of full-time jobs at a large university in the city I was moving to after graduation. Of those nearly 50 applications I submitted, I received phone interviews for just two positions. Both were entry-level positions (bachelor's degree required) and had salary postings lower than what I was expecting to make after going through the work to get my master's degree. However, I didn't have any connections or acquaintances at the university, and I realized that I couldn't be picky since I was moving to that city upon graduation regardless of whether I had a job. After two interviews, I was offered a position as an Admissions Counselor for the university, which I happily accepted. I was relieved to have a job in the field I wanted to work in. I know that opportunity is not always afforded.

The university where I was fortunate enough to begin my professional career is a very large institution. To accommodate the large number of students we were tasked to recruit to the university, my team consisted of about 20 Admissions Counselors. For the most part, all of us were on the same level when it came to job responsibilities and salary. A few of us already had our master's degree, but the majority did not (some were working toward it). For most, this was just a stop on the way to the job and career they really wanted, which often wasn't in Higher Education. For me though, this opportunity was a crucial step in the ladder on my way to a satisfying professional career working at the university. I took my responsibilities seriously and worked to always perform my job duties to the best of my ability. I enjoyed the work I was doing but felt that something was missing. I wanted to do more.

After a short time in this position, I found that simply performing my job duties would not make me stand out among my peers who were all doing the same thing. I knew that I needed to go a step beyond being a good employee, and be an employee that management would think toward if an opportunity for a promotion ever became available. So, I began doing things to establish myself as a leader on our team. I volunteered to attend extra college fairs and would always make myself available whenever management had last-minute requests of the team. Most importantly, I worked to establish deeper relationships with our leadership team and brought them ideas I had to improve various aspects of the department. Through all of this, I purposefully kept my newly discovered leadership brand in mind. I had become an unofficial leader among my co-workers who would always step in to help when there was a need. That's how my peers and leadership team came to know me.

This transformational journey taught me the importance of servant leadership in the workplace. When I began my professional career, I assumed that my advanced degree would signal quick promotions into established leadership roles. However, in a competitive workplace with job requirements that prioritized efficiency and tangible production, I eventually learned that breaking the mold by working outside of the job description is not just an altruistic trait, but one that is valued by all levels of management. My hard work was rewarded when I was promoted to Coordinator Senior of Early Recruitment after one year of being an Admissions Counselor. My management team saw potential in me after I had gone above and beyond to serve the greater good of our department, and gave me the chance that I had been seeking since completing my master's degree one year earlier.

In this newly created position, I was able to develop recruitment programs for my department that focused on educating 9th, 10th, and 11th grade high school students (a demographic that had not gotten as much attention in the past) about college preparation. As an individual now in an official leadership position, it would have been easy for me to hang my hat on the fact that I now had this title and not be as involved in the work activities that others in similar positions may have seen as "beneath them" (I think we have all encountered at least one person like this). However, that mindset was not part of my leadership brand that I had worked so hard to establish, and not a way that I would ever want to treat my team. So, I remained very involved in the day-to-day operations of our department, including stepping up to help whenever needed as I had done before my promotion, while also establishing myself in my new position by taking on more responsibilities. And you know what? My team was willing to help me out when I needed them because I had always done the same for them. That is the essential core of servant leadership.

So yes, you do often need to pay your dues, and you may have to start at the bottom and work your way up the ladder. And that is not a bad thing. I learned so much on my way up to earning a leadership position, and I will take those lessons with me into my future leadership and career opportunities. I learned that I am not owed anything, and it is important to put 110% into my work regardless of which stage of my career I am in. Starting in a position with room for growth allowed me to really establish my identity in the workplace and discover the leadership style that allows me to best serve any team I find myself a part of. Every opportunity, no matter how small, is a chance to learn and grow as a leader. Seize it!

***

Carly is a Higher Education Professional who has worked in Admissions and Recruitment at multiple universities, and currently serves as an Academic Success Specialist at a large public university. She enjoys helping students map out their college experience and ensure that they have the tools they need to be successful in college and beyond. When she's not working, she enjoys spending time with her husband and dog and watching movies.

The Gift Guru

Who would have thought that a slow cooker would dictate my level of success as the National Promotions Manager for Caesars Entertainment? Right as I was promoted into this role, my boss told me that I needed to develop an action plan to consolidate promotional gift purchasing and become the main contact for overseas orders. Bam!

I had no idea where to even begin, but my mind drifted to my first promotional gift giveaway where I had a lengthy, detailed conversation with a dissatisfied guest. During this interaction, the guest explained to me that this no-name slow cooker was cheap and that it would probably break before exiting the casino and landing in his kitchen cabinet. The truth was that I didn't completely disagree with the guest, and I didn't want to draw attention to the fact that we actually paid extra for the white and grey chevron print design. For the remainder of the event, I was left to battle the crowd of angry guests with service recoveries galore that ranged from buffet vouchers to casino play.

I left my boss' office knowing that the road to success would be paved with name brand gifts. I had to develop a plan that would provide the best gift, at the best price to drive cost savings. I also knew that the Voice of the Customer mattered, and that I needed to select gift choices that fit our customer demographic.

Obviously my first gift of choice would be a slow cooker. I owed that to the hundreds of disappointed guests. I started conversations with vendors all across the United States. I was determined to find the perfect slow cooker, so I requested close to 20 samples to be delivered to my office. Guess what? Quart size matters. And, so does the color, design, and material of choice. Then, because I apparently have expensive taste, I selected the one slow cooker that was clearly out of my budget. But it was beautiful. And, it wasn't a matter of want. It was a matter of need. So I did what any person would do. I catapulted myself outside of my comfort zone, channeled my street market skills from a vacation in Costa Maya, Mexico and started price negotiating.

I was surprised at the person I had become, but I wasn't mad about it. Fifty cents off the asking price would simply not do. I was looking to save George Washingtons! (I was determined to save money), and with each phone call and email to the vendor, I kept that one angry guest in the front of my mind. At one point, I recall telling the vendor that I needed her to be my fairy godmother and make this happen. This would be the beginning of a great partnership if she could just understand my slow cooker debacle of 2012 and cut me a deal. At first, I had a little bit of anxiety asking for such a big discount, but then I realized that I needed to make my mark in the vendor world and make her realize that there was only one of me and many more of her. Five confident phone calls later, I sealed the deal!

Now, this slow cooker wasn't special because it was dipped in gold or had a fancy design. The significance of this hand selected, name branded slow cooker is what made this gift superior to any other gift that had ever been given out to our casino guests. This slow cooker was the perfect tailgate tagalong at the next family football outing, and it was mine – $3.00 cheaper than the original asking price and under budget.

I was ready to submit my order for 15,000 slow cookers total, but I simply could not do it alone. During this part of the process, I learned the importance of patience and deadline awareness. As an overseas order, the factory would be making these slow cooker solely for me, but they wouldn't dare start production until I submitted the order. That's how the business works! Therefore, I worked with a group of employees to determine all of the casino specific information such as quantity, event date, and loading dock details. Then, after all information was confirmed and finalized, I submitted the orders for fifteen participating casinos, located in various parts of the United States.

My next step was to anxiously wait as my

complete order was mass produced overseas. I felt good about my first company-wide order, but I knew it wasn't over yet. As the first event date neared, I began communicating with the vendor requesting tracking information for the property shipments, and prayed to the gift gods that each slow cooker giveaway was one hundred times better than my experience

So what did I learn along the way? Working for a hospitality driven company, I have learned the balance of a great leader is to understand the company's goals while keeping the guest experience intact. Never be afraid to take on new responsibilities because there is something satisfying about implementing a new idea or concept that works and has a successful impact on the company. Being a Project Manager for a new concept equals a lot of trial and error. I had to ask a lot of questions, but I also felt empowered to make important decisions without guidance. I had to be okay with constructive criticism, allowing my process to continuously be modified along the way, always keeping the guest experience in front of my mind. I quickly learned to be the voice of my company and to not be afraid to demand cheaper pricing, within reason. My process has been implemented for over a year, and I have saved the company over $2 million dollars. That's a lot of slow cookers!

Every time I start the gift ordering process, I think back to the day where the guest demanded a better gift, and I strived to make that happen. I want the Promotion Associates working the gift giveaway to feel proud, like Rafiki from the Lion King presenting Simba to the herd, as they hold out that prized gift to the guest and say, "Welcome to Caesars, Mr. Jones. Here is your Hamilton Beach Slow Cooker, perfect for dips, pot roasts, and chili.

Enjoy your gift."

***

Jessica started her career in the gaming industry at Harrah's New Orleans & moved to Las Vegas two years later to work in Corporate Marketing, planning Special Events for Caesars Entertainment. Although she misses crawfish boils, Saints games in the Super Dome, & Southern hospitality, she embraces the fast-paced Las Vegas lifestyle. When she's not cooking, hiking, or making homemade wine, she fills her spare time with weekend adventures, community service, & networking events.

Jessica is a member of Sigma Sigma Sigma Sorority, Las Vegas Junior League, & Krewe of King Arthur. She received her BA in 2007 & her MA in 2009, both from Southeastern Louisiana University.

Shortly after writing her submission, Jessica was offered a position as an Account Executive for Eagle Promotions, where she now sells slow cookers to the casino industry.

The Teacher

Many believe that leadership is an inherent part of the job we call teacher, granted automatically by its title. In other words, children are told upon entering school to respect and defer to their teachers, as they possess the authority of their classrooms. We all have pictures in our heads of students immediately greeting the entering teacher with a communal "Good Morning Mrs. . . . " who will faithfully lead her students through the lessons, challenges, and accomplishments of the day. Her end goal: student success!

So what does student success mean? And what does leading that classroom look like? What traits should this leader have? Because each classroom, year after year, can be so divergent from its previous, I believe there is no one success model for a classroom or a teacher. I would never prescribe a certain way to do things; I can only tell you what worked over the years for me.

First, be fair.

Don't we just hate it when kids cry the "that's not fair" anthem—we often quickly retort, "well, the world's not fair!" Precisely why we should strive to bring fairness to our classroom. Have clearly defined expectations and stick to them. Make them achievable for all and insist on meeting them. Does this mean everyone gets an A? Oh no no. That would not be fair. Fair is impartial and honest—it conforms to the established rules. If you map out clearly what your students must do to be successful, they, themselves, will know if they achieve it and to what degree, and they will not hide behind, "well, Mrs. . . . just isn't fair." In the end, students really want to be rewarded for reaching and achieving—no one really wants that trophy for just breathing!

Second, be strict.

Now I don't mean live by the motto "my way or the highway" or to have a punitive approach to consequences —you are working with growing human beings and as such kindness and compassion should permeate your classroom environment. What I mean is, have clear and well-defined boundaries for how you expect your students to act, do work, and treat others and do not cross those boundaries—You, as their guide, do likewise. Hold yourself to a high standard; in turn, students perceive this and will aspire to hold themselves to a higher standard too. You, their leader, should be on time, be prepared, be organized, be timely in your grading, give feedback, be professional, etc. You cannot demand of your students anything you, yourself, is not willing to do.

Last, care.

You must truly care that each and every one of your students who sit before you are there. You must care that she does well, improves, and thrives. You must care that he cares too. YOU are the motivator! I have often heard, “hey, you can’t care more than so-and-so does!” But I think you can. It was never ok for me to accept that adage about . . . if you reach just one that’ll be a success. Hell no—I wanted to reach them all—I wanted every student to love *Hamlet* and use the semi-colon correctly. I wanted every student to cite all sources in perfect MLA style and write beautiful, succinct thesis statements. This is what drives you—to get them ALL!

Of course you’ll always have those complainers, those naysayers, those ‘w-h-a-t-e-v-e-r’ types? How do you choke all that down? It is easy to lead when all goes well, when that class loved the presentation and time flew because the discussion was so robust. It is not so easy when you’ve explained the same thing over and over again over the course of an entire week and in the end Johnny fails the test anyway. Work with it! Maybe it was you, maybe it was Johnny, but maybe you’ll both do better next time.

Teaching, like leadership, is not an exact science. It can’t be—you are leading, working with human beings—never predictable, always challenging, ever changing , and very exciting. Just keep going to June and then live for September!

***

First and foremost, I am a wife, mother of three children, and grandmother of two beautiful granddaughters. I have spent my life in education, teaching high school (mostly seniors) English in subjects ranging from English 9-12, Mass Media, AP English Literature, and Public Speaking. I now am a Senior Library Clerk at a community college, still aiding students but not in a classroom. I believe heartily in the value of education but that learning can be achieved in many different ways and should occur everyday, whether that be through observation, interaction, or contemplation, and always through READING! So, read on!

The Paramedic

It was the perfect resuscitation. A video of it could have been used as a training tool showing how everything is supposed to go. Everyone was in their place, the physician, the nurses, the paramedic, the registration clerk, the chaplain, and the child life specialist. Every piece of equipment was in perfect working order, in exactly the proper place and ready to go when the child came through the door. It was perfect. Textbook perfect. And yet… the child died.

As a paramedic, you see the best and the worst of the world and people. There are good days and there are… well days like that fateful one. Days that you wish you had a do-over. Days that you wish would never happen again.

I remember that day so vividly. Each person knew their role and executed it with precision. The airway was managed, IV lines established, monitors attached, assessment completed, medications administered, labs drawn and sent and CPR started immediately when indicated.

The parents were in the room talking to their child, listening to and watching everything that was happening in the dance of organized chaos. Every single person was on point, performing each task exactly how we had practiced it dozens of times.

It wasn't enough. It just wasn't enough.

We followed our training. We administered world class care. We did everything we were supposed to do.

From an outside perspective the room looked chaotic and destroyed, yet we were in sync. Everyone was dripping with sweat. Each step of the process had gone like clockwork. Nobody missed a beat. It just couldn't be. That's what I kept telling myself. But it was.

We stood there, with tears welling in our eyes, as the child's parents were told, we lost him.

His mother let out the most primal scream of agony imaginable. I'll never forget that sound. Trust me, I've tried. I still have nights where I wake up in a cold sweat, haunted by the sound of that mother's pain.

I have asked myself a million times what could I have done differently. What had I not studied? What had I not practiced? What did I not have in place? What did I miss? Did I fail this child? Did I fail this family? Am I not a good leader? Do I not have the qualities it takes to be one? Was I stupid enough to think I could be? What do I do now?

You can do everything right, by the book, follow all the training and education you have been given and still you lose. The child dies. The parents are shattered. Your soul is never the same.

It took me a very long time to find any semblance of good from that day. Trying to find a silver lining in some clouds can prove to be more difficult than others. I finally did though; I learned potentially the most valuable leadership lesson of my life.

Leadership is not always a win. I hate that. I have to accept it, but I refuse to ever like it. As a mother and grandmother, I know that I can't stop now. I have two options: allow that terrible day to stop me from doing my work or allow it to push me to fight harder, to think more critically and to keep saving lives.

We often tell ourselves to hope for the best, but to prepare for the worst. These words bear such greater meaning to me now. I know the value of having a support system there to catch you when you've experienced the worst. If I could leave you with one lesson, it would be to allow yourself to grieve and process in those times where leadership is not a win, but eventually find that silver lining and use it to reach your greatest heights.

***

Lisa Grulke is originally from Middle Amana, Iowa and was born to Bill and Audrey Metz. She attended Northeast Missouri State University (now Truman State University) where she met her husband Dennis Grulke. She and Dennis have 5 children and 8 grandchildren, but Lisa serves as a mother figure to many of her students as well.

Lisa has held many roles in her career. She began working as a paramedic in the pediatric emergency room at Blank Children's Hospital in 1999. She began her teaching career as an EMT instructor for Des Moines Area Community College in 2000. Shortly after starting this teaching role, she chose to attend Drake University where she finished her Bachelor's degree in 2005. Lisa has served (and continues to serve) as a biology lab instructor for more than a decade.

The Fashionista

I was nearing my junior year of high school and remember sitting in my room alone thinking "What do I want to do? And how am I going to do it?"

I was just a girl from Rochester who liked fashion… like hundreds of other girls did. I didn't think I was overly talented or gifted. It's not like I could draw a sketch of a proportioned body in a gown – let alone a stick figure. But I did know it's what I wanted to TRY to do. Since I wasn't as good with the creative or design side, I wanted to make it in the business end of the industry. I was always good at taking initiative to go after what I wanted, and I knew it was in me but I didn't know how I was going to get there.

After following some advice from people I loved, I got a job working alongside the proprietor of a boutique while in high school. After completing high school, I pursued a major in fashion merchandising and worked at the boutique when I was home for breaks. During my time there, I learned the selling and buying end of retail and got to accompany the owner to NYC trade shows. She taught me the in's and out's of how to run a small retail business and I always held that information in my back pocket. It was there, at one of the tradeshows, that I met people who would be my future co-workers at Steve Madden.

I began my time at Steve Madden interning, while still in college. I never thought little old me, the "homebody" could live in NYC, but the internship taught me to step up to the plate and stop complaining because, frankly, nobody cared. I got used to the physical and emotional stress that comes with the industry. Whether it was packing bags of shoes, getting coffee orders yelled at me, or learning how to enter orders on a computer system from the 80's, interning gave me the opportunity to work with various departments. It's where I acquired skills that helped me see through the entire fashion cycle. I knew I needed to finish my senior year of college in New York, and at the best place for fashion- FIT (Fashion Institute of Technology). I thought, let me finish school in New York and I can always come home, be close to my family, and work a fashion job in Rochester. WRONG!

Luckily I enjoyed my senior year in the concrete jungle and started applying for big girl jobs in NYC. I decided I was staying. I was hired immediately after graduation as Wholesale Sales Coordinator at Steve Madden. I was in this position for longer than I wanted to be. I thought moving up would be easy... that I would come across. I then realized I had to keep taking initiative to get where I wanted. I would work hard, come early, stay late, ask questions, and make sure to put it in peoples ears that I wanted to grow and get into buying.

From there, I was finally tasked with a greater opportunity on the retail side of the company, as an Analyst, to help merchants dig into their business needs. I knew this was another stepping stone and that I would have to prove myself now on the other side of the company. There were times I felt like I had started from scratch and thought "Should I have just stayed in wholesale where I knew everyone and everything?"

Again, I took initiative and spoke to any higher ups I could get a hold of and let it be known that I would do whatever it takes to get into buying. After only 6 months as an analyst I was promoted to my current position as an Assistant Buyer- one of only two for my department. I had finally gotten there. Where I wanted to be.

Or so I thought...

After a year in the position, I learned so many skills, whether it be talking to vendors from Portugal, learning crazy math formulas in excel, or designing samples of shoes, I felt like I did it all.

But what was it for?

Even at a well-established company working a great position, I was still working to live. New York City is not for the boring, the poor, or the naive. I got sick of paying $1300 for a shoe box apartment...And I was never quite drunk enough to spend $18 on a St. Germaine cocktail. (Ok, maybe a few times.) But quite honestly the work became a part of me- it defined me. I would have dreams of my boss yelling "Are we going to make the 4th quarter numbers?!" or "Why the F*** would you do that?"

That's why I've learned to get up and go back home.

Mary Schmich has a well-known quote "Live in New York City once, but leave before it makes you hard. Live in Northern California once, but leave before it makes you soft."

I learned a very valuable lesson in all this: Take initiative. Work hard for what you want, and if you get there and it's not all you hoped it'd be, its ok to change. You never hear someone on their death bed saying "I wish I spent more time at the office!" But I'm sure many people say that they wish they spent more time with the ones they love.

***

Alana Cummings is a Rochester native but lived in New York City for 5 years. After studying Fashion Merchandising at FIT, she interned at Steve Madden, where she later got a job after graduating. She moved her way up from an Account Associate, to a Retail Analyst, to an Assistant Buyer. She recently made the decision to move back to Rochester to be closer to her family and couldn't be happier. She currently works as an Account Executive for a Technology company and is looking forward to where this career will take her.

The Sorority Woman

I've always found myself in some kind of leadership position. I've been the section editor of the yearbook, member of the student government, an athlete, and the president of multiple clubs. None of that compared to being a two-term sorority president. On top of that, we were a brand new chapter and I was leading us all into unchartered territory. Talk about pressure. But I'm so grateful for those two years.

As you can imagine, leading other strong and accomplished woman can be both thrilling and intimidating. We wanted to raise the bar of what it meant to be a sorority woman on campus, while also seeking acceptance by our peers. What good is a community program if no one comes to it? It was my job to manage the many personalities in the chapter, as well as build relationships with other fraternity and sorority leaders on campus.

You see there were some individuals in the chapter who just made it difficult for us to do anything. They worked hard to convince everyone to do things their way, which distracted us from our goals. Now don't get me wrong, we were able to accomplish great things and won several awards during my terms, but I struggled standing up to the louder voices in the room.

Despite all of my accomplishments and previous leadership positions, I wasn't comfortable with making waves that I felt would negatively impact our group dynamic. As a group of women starting a new sorority on campus, we had formed a bond by overcoming many obstacles. This included being ostracized by our peers from time to time. I didn't want the added challenge of not being accepted by my own sisters and roommates.

Well, after a year of restoring relationships and gaining the support of our peers throughout my first term, one of my sorority sisters continued to start drama. Out of what I thought was loyalty, I continued to defend her and make excuses for her behavior. The straw that broke the camel's back came when she began to lie and put members of the chapter into compromising situations. Specifically, it started creating friction between the organizations we were previously isolated by. I had to decide what was more important – my perceived loyalty to one person or the reputation and longevity of my sorority on campus. I chose the sorority. My sorority sister was not happy about that, and I began to see people treat me differently. She was able to convince others in the chapter that I couldn't be trusted.

There came a time that if a conversation didn't involve the sorority or paying bills, that I was left out. After a few months, it took a heavy toll on me emotionally. Here I was being pushed away from a group of women that I called sisters and struggled with to bring our sorority to campus. I started to lose sight of why I joined and who I was long before the joining. I was a loving cheerful person that always smiled and lent a helping hand. I wasn't a recluse that cried herself to sleep feeling like I had to face the world alone.

One day I came home from hanging out with friends to hear some my sorority sisters negatively talking about them. I decided right then and there that I was worth the conflict. I joined their conversation and demanded respect. They said they were concerned that I was naïve and allowing people they didn't approve of to manipulate me against them. I told my sisters that I was more than capable of choosing my own friends and was willing to learn what ever lessons that came along with that decision. I shared the disappointment and hurt that I was feeling from their recent behavior towards me. I told them that I was no longer going to let them have power over how I felt about myself, and that their disrespect of me would no longer be tolerated. They were taken aback at first, and as the conversation continued they acknowledged the behavior and apologized. As time passed, our relationship improved and I had my respect from them, but more importantly from myself. A few months later they elected me for a second term as president.

After being able to stand up for myself, I saw my

confidence and self-esteem improve. I wasn't concerned about pleasing everyone to be popular or avoid conflict, but I wanted to set a good example and do what was right.

Being a leader means having the courage to stand firm in your convictions. At times, this will mean demanding your respect. Who doesn't want to be liked by the people they work with? We all do, but that doesn't mean everyone shares the same belief system in what is best for the greater good or how we treat one another. As I've shared, doing what is right isn't always popular, or come without backlash. But I grew stronger in who I was as a woman and a leader.

It's like the popular saying goes; "you can't pour into others from an empty cup." Good leadership requires loving yourself and those you lead, but that can't happen if you're not taking care of yourself. You can't give someone else joy when you don't have any. Placing our holistic health – emotional, spiritual, physical, etc. – as a priority is important and also takes courage. It took a lot of tears, hard lessons and counseling to understand my worth and value. Once I understood it, I wasn't going let anyone take it from me. Don't get me wrong, there are times where I still struggle with this, but I always come back to my faith that reminds me that there is a divine purpose placed on my life and that I am worthy of living in that purpose.

Finally, this opened my eyes to the biggest lesson that most fraternity and sorority members learn. All sisters/brothers aren't meant to be your friends, and all friends aren't meant to be your sisters/brothers. I learned that just because we were sorority sisters and were initiated together, that did not automatically make us friends. Like any other relationship, friendship and sisterhood requires work. I had to help others learn to separate Shanté the chapter president (leader), and Shanté their friend. Once there was understanding of the difference, our ability to work together grew into a true life-long friendship.

***

Shanté Hearst is the Assistant Director of Fraternity & Sorority Life at Texas A&M University, and a member of Delta Sigma Theta Sorority, Inc. She takes pride in modelling the way for her students, applying the lessons she has learned to help them become better leaders prepared to face the challenges life will bring.

The Fraternity Man

When Jordan asked me if I would write an excerpt for his book on leadership, I thought to myself, "why me?" I was the founding colony president of a leadership development fraternity as well as the chaplain (brotherhood chair) but other than meeting the typical expectations, what kind of leader was I? As I reflect on those times, I realize that there are just as many lessons to be learned from when I fell short as a leader as from when I succeeded.

Prior to the fraternity as an undergraduate, I had zero experience as a leader. Zilch. Nada. It was not until Jordan and I spoke about the potential future implications on my life, if I were not to take a position in leadership, that I truly realized what an opportunity was before me. I had never had the opportunity to lead something, nor may I ever have had such an opportunity again. Little did I know just how much my role as president would affect my life as a leader and as a person. There is a recurring theme that continues to come to mind as I reflect on the fraternity and how my life has changed. It is best described by a quote from a pastor, Andy Stanley, "direction, not intention determines your destination." Three things that had an effect on my direction were my vision, my actions, and my beliefs (more specifically, my belief in myself and others). All three of these were significantly altered as a result of my fraternity experience.

My best friend and I had said since starting college that fraternity life was not for us, but when he caught wind that a new fraternity would be starting on campus, he said we should check it out. I immediately began to envision the benefits that starting a fraternity would bring: popularity, business connections, job opportunities, etc. So, right from the start my intentions and direction seemed aligned. What I did not know at the time was that when I accepted my position as president that my best friend, who became vice president, would suddenly become complacent.

The issue was that for the six years that we had known each other, he had always been more of the leader of our wolf pack, and now that the roles had reversed, he did not know how to take it, and, to be honest, neither did I.

When I first considered a position of leadership within the fraternity, I failed to see my own potential as a leader due to my lack of experience, lack of belief in myself, and simple acceptance of the way things were. I struggled for years prior with my capability of believing in myself, and now I was faced with the challenge of leading this organization without my best friend's support. It was always easier for me to accept the decisions of confident individuals, like my friend, than to be my own decision maker, but as fate would have it, I was not meant to go the easy way.

Due to the fact that the vice president was also my very good friend and roommate, I spent much of my time trying to repair our relationship. Thanks to my awareness of our fraternity's long-term goal (vision), I realized that placing all my effort towards binding up a wound that I did not inflict was only hindering our advancement. His efforts were focused on trying to unite the brothers by eliminating those that were different, so that we all fit a certain image. This is something I just knew was wrong. We did not join fraternities before because we wanted to be different, and if this was the case, why on earth were we trying to make everyone the same? This was a clear indication for me that I needed to stand up for myself, for others, as well as for what I believed in. While the original vision for the fraternity kept me going, the falling out with my close friend hindered my belief in the capabilities of others as well as my trust in them.

I continued to speak up for those who rarely spoke up for themselves; now I realize I should have given them a voice instead of being theirs. It was hard enough trying to get 45 college age men to listen to someone that they see as their friend rather than their leader, but I seemed to only make matters worse. Although we did have many complacent members in our fraternity who would have rather partied than improve, I over-generalized to the majority of the fraternity. I no longer saw the capability in the men that were willing to do what needed to be done. In order to become officially recognized by the national fraternity and perpetuate our advancement to chapter status, we had a list of requirements that we had to reach. I began to micromanage members of my organization, which I believe I did out of my desire to protect the interests of the vision shared with me from the national fraternity. I would sit down for long periods of time with almost every brother with some level of responsibility and personally show him how to do his job. There is nothing wrong with teaching someone how to do their job, but I seemed to go a step too far by doing their job for them, which resulted in the vicious circle of them becoming complacent regardless. The combination of consistent support for the little guys with quiet voices and the micromanaging of the majority with the big voice caused me to have a hard time gaining the long-term support of new members coming in.

My focus was still on trying to create order among the chaos of the upper ranks by creating a shared vision. My intention was to create a vision of equality among everyone within the chapter, but in doing so, my actions led to the appearance that I favored one group over another. I found that an important thing to do when cultivating the vision of the organization was to meet the members on their level, and as a leader to help them see their potential at my level. In my eyes, my goal was to help members visualize that their status was a temporary state and that they could reach greater potential through motivation. The thing is that I still had so much to learn at that time about myself and about leadership.

Coming down to their level meant that I might end up compromising more of my image as a leader than I truly wanted. The more time that I spent there the more that I was seen as a friend and the less I was visualized as a leader. Despite my track record within the fraternity as president, which included being reelected as well as helping the fraternity to gain its charter, the brothers did not like being micromanaged or taking instruction from someone they saw more as a friend. This led eventually to a bit of a falling out and one of my greatest challenges within the fraternity.

The biggest takeaway, for me is twofold. One, is that there is a clear difference between helping others find their voice and becoming their voice. Your job as a leader is to do the former, not the latter. The second lesson I learned was to understand that as a leader sacrifices must be made. You simply can't be liked by everyone, nor can you expect to be appreciated by everyone. It's important to remember that you were put into leadership for a reason. Whether you were elected or you were the first to step up, you need to know you have the strength to succeed.

***

Growing up in the small city of Friendswood, Texas, Austin Gerland always knew he was destined to go places other than the fast food joint in the center of town. Due to his close relationship with his family and the unexpected loss of his older brother, he decided to put his traveling itch on hold for another year after high school.

After attending community college close to home for a year, he stepped out a bit to attend school at the

University of Texas at San Antonio (UTSA). There he gained a double major in Marketing and Psychology.

During his time at UTSA, he joined Alpha Tau Omega Fraternity, in which he led the new colony to reestablish its charter as the founding president and later as the chaplain. He attributes his strive for camaraderie and success within the chapter to the memory of his brother. As his time at UTSA came to an end, Austin sought to take his mantra "People with big dreams live big lives" seriously, and he pursued work overseas.

After months of searching and nearly losing hope, he landed a marketing internship in Karlsruhe, Germany where he currently lives. Since moving there in 2015, he has learned German, acted in a German musical, and begun a career as a foreign languages teacher. His hobbies include acting, traveling, staying involved in his church, and spending quality time with his friends in Germany, who have become like his adopted family.

The Debate Coach

When I became the head coach of an intercollegiate speech and debate team in the summer of 2013, I decided that I needed a guiding and overarching principle that drove my leadership style and set the proper tone with my squad. I eventually settled on a quote by famous Irish political theorist Edmund Burke: "the only thing necessary for the triumph of evil is for good men to do nothing." I prided myself on upholding the ethos of this quotation at all times. I recruited multiple LGBTQ students to the team, which is extremely rare for our campus, a Christian institution that is known for its conservative theological belief system. I was elected president of our organization at 26 years old, which made me the youngest president of a regional speech and debate organization in the country. I also opened my students' eyes by having them read books by critical race and gender scholars like bell hooks and Michel Foucault. However, in my rush to pat myself on the back for being a groundbreaking "social justice warrior" I overlooked patterns of behavior that were deeply affecting my students in competition, and it nearly tore my team apart. What I learned led me on a journey to change the fundamental structure of speech and debate in our region.

The majority of my team (like my institution) is female. I make note of this because it is extremely rare for speech and debate teams to be populated largely by women. Scholars in the field are finding that complicated socio-cultural issues at play (which mirror larger social norms) cause women to experience more issues than men in speech and debate competition. Recent research found that women are quickly increasing their participation in speech and debate, but are achieving far less success than their share of the total competitor population would indicate (Furgerson & Rudnick, 2014). Currently, there is a 20% gap between the amount of women who compete in the activity compared to those who advance to elimination rounds in those events (Donovan, 2012). This is due in part to the way that women are perceived in competition. Debate judges viewed "assertive" men as demonstrating positive behaviors, while women who displayed those same attributes were viewed negatively (Matthews, 2015). Even more problematic, female competitors report experiencing verbal, physical, and sexual physical harassment at a higher rate than the average female college student (Stepp, 2001). As a male former competitor and coach, I didn't pay attention to these inequities, and for a long time did not view them with much urgency. This began to change in the fall of 2015, when two of my female debaters – Jenny and

Tiffany - came to me in tears and stated that one of their male opponents began mocking them in-round. I asked them to expand on their complaint and Tiffany explained how the competitor repeated the arguments she and Jenny made earlier, but then proceeded to raise his voice to an extremely high pitch and use exaggerated hand gestures as a way to de-legitimize them. This continued for almost three minutes straight. When Tiffany finished describing what transpired, I immediately told them "don't be bothered by a knucklehead who acts half his age, rise above the fray." As someone who played sports throughout my childhood, I felt this was appropriate advice any of my youth baseball or basketball coaches would have told me in a similar situation. However, both Tiffany and Jenny immediately acted shocked at my nonchalant response. Not thinking much of this at the time, I brushed it off.

Unfortunately, two tournaments later, the issue reached a breaking point. Early on in the competition, a third female debater on my team - Allison - approached me in tears and stated that the same male debater openly mocked her in round in a similar way he did to Tiffany and Jenny. Thinking that same approach worked before, I repeated the same advice to Allison. As the tournament reached the final round, a fourth female debater of mine - Karen - qualified to the final round where she would face the now infamous opponent. At this point, my team was now concerned that this pattern of behavior would continue. To give her moral support, I instructed four of her teammates to be in the room and watch the round. When it finished, I saw Karen leave in tears. I approached my team and asked what happened. They told me Karen mispronounced the term "Keynsian economics" in one of her speeches, and he then spent nearly two minutes in his rebuttal arguing that since she couldn't pronounce the word, it shows that she doesn't have the intellect to be making these arguments. He finished his diatribe by stating "she's making women debaters look bad by arguing concepts that are above her capacity to understand." Stunned by this revelation, I approached the male debater and demanded he apologize to Karen for his actions. He sheepishly apologized to me and promised me that he would talk to Karen. I then went to the tournament director and told him what had taken place throughout the competition, and I also demanded that the student be reprimanded for his actions. The tournament director, who has been a coach in the community for over 20 years, told me that this type of stuff happens all the time. He further noted that this is a product of young, immature students who act emotionally and will eventually learn as they compete longer. I asked if there is a protocol in place to take action, to which he responded that it was up to him. Unsurprisingly, he declined to hand down any punishment.

As I walked away in disbelief, Jenny, Tiffany, Allison, and Emily (one of our female assistant coaches) pulled me aside and asked to have a private conversation. Over the next 45 minutes they explained that women have uniquely faced this type of abuse since they began competing in greater numbers, and that it continues because women lack positions of power or authority to enact change. At the end, Emily finished the conversation by saying to me "Barry, we know your heart is in the right place, but we are saddened that after seeing this happen so many times, you merely responded by asking us to 'toughen up.' Debaters who engage in misogynistic and sexist behavior will continue to wreak havoc on women who are trying to find their voice if we continue to enable their actions by not holding them truly accountable. The key is educating them on why their conduct is problematic. As the president, you can do something about this. We've been waiting for you take action."

When Emily was done, I stood silent in place for several minutes, contemplating what had just happened. As I began piecing together all of the events from the past year, I realized just how right they were. An overwhelming majority of head coaches, and every single tournament director in our community were older men. The ability for women to give voice to their experiences were mitigated by their lack of positions of power. However, more pressing to me is how I had failed as the head coach of the team to be a true advocate for a demographic of debaters that had experienced so much pain, discrimination, and emotional abuse. I basked in the glory of winning trophies, breaking barriers at our school, but stood silent when a large portion of my team felt that I had let them down when they needed me most. My lack of interest in trying to empathize with the experience of my female competitors kept me blind to their reality. It was at that moment I thought back to Edmund Burke. Now was the time for me be a true advocate and take action.

As I mulled my next steps, I reached out to current and former female competitors and coaches. Each of them relayed a strikingly similar message: help organize women and give them the ability to vote on changes to the way the organization operates. After doing more research, I did just that. I am proud that during the past three months, I have helped put together a group of women who will be presenting a three part proposal at our organization's annual conference in September, which includes the following:

1. The creation of a sexual harassment advisory board that will serve as a check on the unilateral power of the tournament director.

2. Hiring a Title IX coordinator that will be present at each tournament.

3. The implementation of a "three strikes" policy for students and coaches/judges who commit any form of harassment.

4. A sexual harassment training program that all violators will need to take before participating in more tournaments.

Although the issues of sexual assault and harassment run deeper than speech and debate, I believe that the more intercollegiate clubs, organizations, and teams join forces to implement concrete policies, the easier it is to cultivate an inclusive, positive environment for marginalized groups of students. This whole ordeal not only gave me a new perspective on leadership, but on the meaning of Edmund Burke's celebrated quote. For good to triumph, men should not just act alone. They should take action that will empower everyone around them to create long-lasting change for all.

*names and some details have been changed to protect identities

***

Barry is a Professor of Speech Communication at Central Arizona College. Barry's scholarly interests include the history of intercollegiate forensics, sports communication, and the intersection of political rhetoric, gender, and race. He is passionate about increasing cultural and intellectual diversity in Speech and Debate, Greek life, and other higher education extracurricular activities.

References

Donovan, K. (2012). The success gap. National Forensic Journal, 30(1), 42-46.

Furgerson, J., & Rudnick, J. (2014). Putting the gender in" gender parity": Breaking new methodological ground in the debate over gender equity in forensics. Forensic, 99(2), 1-19.

Matthews, N. C. (2015). The influence of biological sex on perceived aggressive communication in debater–judge conflicts in parliamentary debate. Western Journal of Communication, 80(1), 1-22.

Stepp, P. L. (2001). Sexual harassment in communication extra-curricular activities: Intercollegiate debate and individual events. Communication Education, 50(1), 34-50.

The SGA President

If greatness was defined by my bossy and firm nature as a child, then you could say I was destined for greatness. I wasn't spoiled per-se, but I lived by my own rules. It didn't occur to me when I was little that I was the so-called leader of the group. It just felt natural to make decisions and always have a plan.

When I was four, my parents got a divorce. That was the first major situation I can remember not being able to control. Surprisingly, I wasn't overly distraught. I think a part of it was that I was so young that comprehending what was happing wasn't limited but more so I think I knew that while I couldn't control the divorce, I could control my own happiness.

Fast forward to high school. During these crucial years of learning I found my true groove as a student leader. I joined Student Council and fell in love with the experience. I was able to impact change and make decisions that benefitted the entire student body.

I learned early on, that sometimes decisions need to be made for the betterment of the group as a whole rather than the success of one. I never ran for Student Body President, because I knew that the role of Second Vice President was a better fit for me. I also knew that leadership isn't just about titles and that the journey dictated the success of our community more than the label on our nametags.

When I enrolled at the University of Nevada, Las Vegas (UNLV) I knew that I wanted to continue pursuing my passion in student government. I was honored to serve as the Vice President for the UNLV Student Government (Consolidated Students of the University of Nevada, Las Vegas or CSUN) because my election proved that others were placing their trust in me.

After countless hours of work and a tireless campaign I was later elected CSUN President. It was in this role that I learned the most about myself, and the most powerful leadership lesson thus far in my career.

Let me be clear, the role was fulfilling but the job wasn't easy. You find yourself growing up really quickly when more than 20,000 students are depending on you.

Sure, there were times I had to pose for photo ops,

kiss babies and whatnot but there were tough times too. Aside from budgeting the finances for students, activities, school and my own personal life, I managed our entire staff.

We had a Director who was difficult from the start. I tried mediation, one on one meetings, formal warnings, and everything else I could think of. None of it helped. My efforts were in vain. Because the salary of CSUN staff is paid by student fees, I knew that I couldn't allow her to keep cashing checks while underperforming.

When I was faced with the reality, that I had to let her go, I was very careful to plan exactly how it needed to happen. As if confronting a friend who isn't performing their job well wasn't hard enough, her godfather was a Regent on the Board of Regents. You know, the people who wrote my paychecks!

I firmly believe that a leader cannot be afraid to make tough decisions. People grow every day, but it's not always for the best. It's our job as peers and leaders to help ensure they are growing positively.

I try to always assess a situation and then place people and things where they will thrive. Recognizing the difference between talents and passions helps me to maximize the strength of organizations or groups I am leading. Someone may love to play the flute but it's difficult for others to listen because they lack talent. Someone else may be the best flautist but it's painful for them to perform because it's not their passion. Similar situations arise in working relationships. You need to find a healthy balance between the two for everyone.

Sometimes I view life as a puzzle and leadership is

the act of piecing it all together. Sometimes the pieces fit perfectly and other times you realize you need to undo much of your work and try again. The important thing to remember is that you need to keep working to complete the never ending puzzle.

***

Kanani Espinoza was born and raised in Las Vegas, NV. She graduated in 2016 from the illustrious William F. Harrah College of Hospitality at the University of Nevada, Las Vegas (UNLV) with a Bachelor's in Hospitality Administration.

As a collegian, Kanani took on many roles. She was the Student Body President for the Consolidated Students of the University of Nevada, Las Vegas (CSUN), was a Founding Member of her sorority - Gamma Phi Beta, and volunteered countless hours to bettering the UNLV and Greater Las Vegas Community.

In the Spring of 2018, she will graduate from the Greenspun College of Urban Affairs at UNLV with her Master's in Public Administration. Kanani currently serves as the President of the Graduate and Professional Student Association (GPSA).

Her passions include helping the Las Vegas community, philanthropy, advising her local Gamma Phi Beta chapter, and staying busy with family, friends, and UNLV events!

The Caregiver

I met Verna, my maternal grandmother only once before the big sit down meeting. I was 10 years old at my great grandmother's estate sale and she sat in a wide recliner and said, "I have every intention of helping you pay for your college education." I didn't really care or understand at the time why this 'absent' family member was making promises to me.

Flash forward 9 years, age 19, by her request, my two siblings and I made the hour drive to discuss at her kitchen table her investments and our future, over a nice bowl of flavorless goulash. She decided that if we were to help her out "a little", she would be willing to share her assets with us when she passed away. We agreed. We didn't know what we had signed up for.

In the years after this meeting, Verna concluded that my siblings were, "useless to her" and that they did not do tasks she would assign them to do to her liking. I convinced her that they were still good people and that they should remain part of her Will. She agreed, but now all of the responsibility fell to me.

To paint you a picture, my grandmother was a filter-less, chain smoking, obese, diabetic opinionated woman with COPD on continuous oxygen who had difficulty walking due to a list of comorbidities. She was so set in her ways that she managed to push virtually all close family and friends away.

For the next 10 years, we were constantly going between the casino and the hospital. This was our life. She really did need more help than just me, but she refused to accept strangers entering her house and would repeatedly say, "I don't want anyone coming in here and taking my stuff." Honestly, she didn't have much of value, just some old smoke-stained clothes and outdated shoes that she said were "beautiful." She always offered me those beautiful shoes; I always declined.

She was very demanding of my time and jealous of anyone else who got it. When this all started I was in my first semester of nursing school and working a full time job at the hospital. She didn't seem to understand that I needed to dedicate my time to studying and other things that 19 year olds do. How could I tell her I didn't have time to do her grocery shopping or take her out of the house when there was no one else to do these things? I couldn't and I didn't. I spent the majority of my time traveling the hour to her house to help her with housework, make sure she got to her Dr.'s appointments and go on outings.

Undeniably, getting her out of the house was difficult. I would help her dress and then we would struggle down the four front stairs together. I would lead her with the walker to her precious Grand Marquis that she insisted we take everywhere because the seats were wide enough. Her favorite place to go was the casino. She was a "chair member", which meant because she spent an enormous amount of money on their slot machines, they would reward her with free night stays, free buffet meals and free shows. She loved free things. She was the richest, cheapest woman I have ever met.

We would get to the casino around 1pm and stay until at least 9pm. On one occasion I fell asleep in her wheelchair next to her favorite nickel machine knowing that I would be tired at work the next day. She woke me up and said, "Danielle, I know you're tired and so am I, but I'm up big and we can't leave yet." I fell back asleep.

When she was winning on the slot machines she would smoke about two cigarettes a minute. We would only take one break, at 4pm, to go to the crab buffet. On two occasions, she ate so much crab that I had to take her home with an upset stomach, and normally she tipped a dollar. When wheeling her away from the table, I would leave the extra tip.

Occasionally, we attended some shows in the Casino event's center. Bobby Vinton and Wayne Newton thrilled her the most, as well as the shopping sprees and the "birthday party" every February for her birthday.

If I didn't come visit and help her when she called she would say, "I take you all these places and pay for all these buffets and you can't even come and see me! You don't even care about me! I am very disappointed in you." It really wouldn't have been right of me to explain to her that these things were not very entertaining for me, that I only did them for her, so I would apologize and arrange to visit the next day.

It wasn't all crab legs and slot machines. Every 3-4 months she could hardly breathe because of her smoking habit and congestive heart failure. I would take her to the hospital in the Grand Marquis, as she would insist that she would not go by ambulance; it cost too much! She would wait in the house uncomfortably for an hour for an hour for me to arrive to take her, but sometimes I would call the ambulance myself. When in the hospital, she would tell nurses and doctors, "This is my granddaughter, she's a registered nurse! Anything you do to me goes through her! She makes all the decisions!" I never remember signing up for this, but I would be at the hospital almost every day when she was admitted. In the end, I did need to make some of the most difficult decisions. She didn't want to live anymore. She would tell me repeatedly, "this is no life to live, I have no quality of life." The last time she was in the hospital she told the doctors she didn't want any more treatment and that she would like to be put in hospice. I respected her decision; however, she didn't seem to understand what that meant. She would constantly say to me, "Why aren't they helping me? I can't breathe! Help me!" The doctors and I would ask her over and over if she was sure she didn't want treatment and she would say yes and refuse treatment. I ended up taking her home with 24-hour care in place, against her wishes, as she said I should be able to provide her with total care. Later, I received a call from the aide service that she passed away 9 hours after I took her home and tucked her into bed for the last time. I told her I loved her and that I would see her in the morning. I did not expect her to pass so soon.

I loved her very much and she loved me although she kept me very busy. It felt good to help someone who needed help although I felt more like a personal aide service than a granddaughter.

As power of attorney at 29 years old, I am now in the process of selling her house and dividing the estate between my siblings. She has in turn set me up for life. I will always be thankful to her for teaching me patience and making me a more compassionate nurse. I can truly relate to my patients and their families better now.

I learned that sometimes in life we are forced to become a leader when we are put into difficult situations that we desperately wish we could avoid. There were times I wanted to scream because I was so frustrated with my grandmother. Other times I would see her name on my caller ID and want to hit ignore.

Today, though, I am grateful for everything she taught me. When a crisis occurs, I am more prepared. When a situation calls for patience, I know I am capable. If I could change one thing, and if I could pass on a message to other caregivers, I'd say, try your best to enjoy each moment you spend with those you are providing care to. Though there may be times that are frustrating and things that irritate you, there will be a time when you'd give anything to have one more of those frustrating days.

***

Danielle Johnson is a Certified Medical-Surgical Registered Nurse (CMSRN) on a high-volume Medical-Surgical unit at Highland Hospital in Rochester, NY.

Prior to nursing, she worked as a patient care technician. Danielle has extensive experience in various environments. She spent time working at Memorial Regional Hospital in Hollywood, FL on a Neurotrauma unit in 2016 before returning to Highland Hospital. She has received multiple nominations for being a Nurse of Excellence in professional development.

She graduated from Bishop Kearney High School and completed her Nursing degree at Monroe Community College. She plans on obtaining an advanced degree in Nursing within the next year with the ultimate goal of working in nursing education.

When Danielle is not at work she loves to exercise, spend time with friends and family and attend sporting events with her dad, who is best known as Pinto Ron.

The Cosmetologist

As you open the door, you are greeted by a bouquet of the week's freshest flowers and a friendly smile. As you wait and sip on your morning coffee, you are consumed with the buzzing noises of blow-dryers and smells of the richest oils and products. People are engaging in conversations about weekend plans and their newest recipes. Men and women are laughing amongst each other and making new friends. A warm happy feeling fills you as you relax and enjoy being taken care of. Welcome to Saturday at our salon.

A very small percentage of people come in and leave like a ship passing through the night. They see our services as a basic necessity and we serve them to the utmost of our ability. But to the greater share of the population, we are so much more.

First, we are hair stylists who bear long hours on our feet, coloring and styling hair, running up and down stairs checking a highlight, doing a haircut in between, grabbing a sip of water while you use the bathroom, applying a conditioning masque on a new client while squeezing in an eyebrow wax. This is the constant race to beat the clock. Every 15 to 30 minutes, more demands, more clients, new needs and new expectations. It will all work out because it must.

Then, we are support systems. We are able to touch and help people in ways many others do not have the capability to do at their jobs. The simple touch and massage of a shampoo can change someone's day or even their week. To some, we are the conversation they are missing with others. We are their network into the newest places to shop, eat, drink, and play. Our tree limbs reach many different elements of our community offering much more than our beauty secrets. Knowing various professionals in so many different fields allows us to recommend and connect our clients and friends with the tools they need to become successful in their personal and professional lives. We are privileged to be able to take care of others.

As hair stylists, we are very giving of ourselves and our time. We love the feeling of helping others feel beautiful on the inside as well as the outside. As they learn from us how to hold their brush as they blow-dry, we learn from them the best way to approach buying a house. As they learn from us which products best suit their hair needs at the moment, we learn from them that sometimes time heals all things and everything happens for a reason. As we walk them out to the front desk with their new-found confidence, their happiness radiates off their face and their kind, complimenting words let us know that all the time we took listening and analyzing what they wished for was worth it. We have given them a special gift with lasting effects. This is the feeling we strive for.

This feeling, however, never comes easy. This business is give and take and there are sacrifices. So much of a hair stylist's day is balance and consistency: being able to look inside yourself to solve someone's needs while still remaining level-headed and secure in yourself. Not every client is a 'knock out of the park' and there are many factors that go into that. Clients are people just like you and me: doctors, nurses, lawyers, scientists, realtors, athletes, and salesmen, with their own internal struggles. Every person has their own set of daily obstacles and sometimes these obstacles interfere with our jobs. It takes a good listener to truly understand that "not happy with my hair" sometimes means "not happy with my spouse" or "not happy with my job" or "the kids are driving me crazy", which complicates our task of pleasing our clients. This becomes an ongoing relationship. If you think about it, we are in the business of making and keeping relationships. We journey through life with people over the years. There are some people with you for a short period of time, while others wouldn't dream of ever leaving for reasons that could be endless and unknown.

Interestingly, as our industry becomes more saturated with cosmetologists, our jobs become harder yet again. The demand to keep up with the latest and greatest of products and techniques increases every day, but knowing the tips and tricks of our trade as well as the scientific breakdown of our products only increases our job security. The average client is much more informed than in the past. It is more important now than ever to challenge ourselves daily so that we can be a better version of ourselves for our clients.

My drive and determination to always better myself within the salon has brought me to another stepping stone in my career. I have become a New York State Ambassador for our salon supporting Goldwell: a global hair color and product company that is distributed locally. I attend extra training and product knowledge classes twice a year and share this knowledge within our salon. There are a small number of us statewide who were chosen to be advocates for increased education of products and better ways to utilize them. This opens many doors for both me and my salon, and success within the salon is success for everyone. The more knowledge that can be harnessed can be used for the greater good and improve of the standards of our service industry.

To be honest, when I first considered a career in the field of cosmetology I didn't know what I was getting myself into. I expected to be cutting, styling and highlighting. The lessons I've learned from my years in the industry have prepared me to lead in every facet of my life. Now as a leader, I know to always listen, really listen, when someone speaks and to look at every situation twice before taking action. What might seem simple at first glance, or what may sound like a simple complaint could actually be the starting point of an unexpected journey

All in all, we have a duty to serve the people. We do our best taking care of them and send them out into the world colored, cut, polished, refreshed, waxed and pinned to perfection - never a hair out of place.

***

As a young girl in elementary school, Brittany had a few school pictures she never wanted to bring home to her parents. Mostly because her father would cut her bangs with kitchen scissors and her mother could barely comb her hair. Getting ready for school every day, she knew she was going to have to learn how to style her own hair and she truly believe this monotonous cycle developed her skills and peaked her interest at a young age to later dive into the field of Cosmetology.

Jumping forward many years later, she is am now a licensed Cosmetologist and has been working full time in the world of Cosmetology for over a decade. Brittany is a Stylist and Color Specialist as well as an Ambassador for Goldwell of New York working as an added connection between her salon and their distributing company. She is always involved in continuing education in her craft for hair coloring services as well as hair cutting and hair styling. The industry is always growing and expanding and she loves that every day is different than the last.

Cosmetologists have the honor of making people look and feel beautiful and every day there are more and more tools to help them do so. Brittany feels truly lucky and thankful for the beauty industry and how it has changed her life. Most of all, she is thankful to her parents, for this head of hair they gave her. Or as she calls it, "her blessing in disguise."

The Small Business Owner

Over the course of a year, it seems like I've experienced it all. Unfortunately I know that will never be the case. What I can say with confidence is the fact that I have learned more in the last year of being a small business owner than I have in my entire professional career.

Prior to leaving my consulting job in Indianapolis, all of my coworkers questioned me for days on end of what my next endeavors might be. To their surprise, my lips remained tightly sealed with only vague clues of where my next steps might lead me. The reason this came as a surprise to most was because I am typically an open book, once you have gotten to know me well enough. However, even some of my closest friends and coworkers did not get the inside scoop until after everything was finalized.

The reason why, you might ask? I knew my next professional step hung on the fate of a 45 second phone call. Not a job offer, but I was waiting to hear back from by phone call. This most certainly was not the case: something bigger. I was waiting to hear back from the U.S. Small Business Administration on whether my business plan and loan proposal had been voted on and whether the vote passed.

Going back a year before that moment, I knew I wanted to be my own boss. I knew I wanted to manage others while also doing something I was truly passionate about. I saw an opportunity in my hometown to return and open a small business that revolved around animal care in the downtown market. We would offer services focused around daytime care, overnight care, and even grooming services, in the Downtown Montgomery, Alabama area. There was no other business remotely similar in the downtown vicinity, everything seemed foolproof: no possible obstacles along the way.

Little did I know that owning a small business might as well be defined as a glorified game of Mario Cart where bananas are thrown at every crossroad. What I mean by this is that no matter how brilliant your idea may be for a business, there are always obstacles along the way. It does not matter how many sleepless nights you have spent "thinking it all out" or how many notations you've placed in your business plan, owning a small business is about being flexible, adaptable, and capable.

This proved true for my business almost immediately upon taking the first step to open. Although I had done plenty of planning, researching, and calculating prior to formation, I consider my first official step toward opening as my search for real estate. To this day, I still remember traveling in my car to Manhattan, Kansas for work when I decided to contact a real estate agent in Montgomery regarding the "perfect commercial property" that I had come across in Downtown Montgomery. Upon answering, I informed the real estate agent that I was a serious buyer who was interested in purchasing commercial property. When I told her the exact address, she kindly informed the property I was referencing was currently under contract. I was crushed.

For somebody who plans everything with precision, my life felt turned upside down instantly. It seemed as though the business could not go on if I was not in that prime piece of real estate. Everything that I envisioned the business might look like came to a screeching halt. However, this future realtor of mine did not see it that way. She was curious to know exactly what I was looking for so she could find me something even better. Within two weeks, she did not simply help me find a better location, she gave me the confidence to move forward realizing I was capable of overcoming any obstacle.

This newly found confidence came in handy not just during the purchasing of the property but also during every other aspect of opening. On top of being flexible with where I saw this business' future location, I mastered the virtue of patience throughout the financing phase, renovation phase, landscaping phase, and even grand opening phase. Although I would have loved to accomplish each milestone by the set date on my calendar, these delays have taught valuable lessons along the way.

First, and most importantly, I could have never succeeded on a personal or professional level without the support of my friends and family. This does not simply extend to the amount of "likes" and comments I received on my social media post announcing that I was opening a business. This level of gratitude is for those who reached out to me personally to cheer me on. Those who sacrificed their spare time on their summer weekends and late nights to help me jackhammer concrete, pull up bushes, lay sod, tear up carpet, paint walls, stain doors, assemble equipment, and even assist with interior décor. The amount of literal blood, sweat, and tears they poured in over the course of four gruesome months will never be forgotten.

Second, provide an experience that is unforgettable to your client. This does not simply guarantee their future business, but it is unpaid marketing for your business. When I first began reaching out to the local Chamber of Commerce about my business plan, I had the opportunity to be mentored by a woman who unknowingly developed our marketing plan in five minutes. Her advice on marketing was to not market. The idea seemed ludicrous at the time, but has been our marketing plan ever since. Her justification behind not marketing was the word of mouth approach. If you provide your clients an unforgettable experience, you have not just earned their continued business, you also have them singing the praise of your business to their own friends, family, neighbors, and coworkers. This in turn, weaves a web of clientele that will last for years to come, assuming you continue to provide them the best experience possible.

Finally, the thought of quitting should never be on your radar. If you are used to things going your way, then you should absolutely not be in the business of owning your own business. If you are easily talked out of something, then chances are good that you were never truly passionate about it to begin with. In turn, this means that you are not willing to devote every waking moment to your business until it is sustainable. After a certain point, you will also learn that quitting may not even be an option. Once you have officially formed the business and invested a certain amount of money into necessary legal issues, building, equipment, and other start- up costs, you will realize there is no backing out. You must be 100% confident that this is what you want before you commit.

Although every business format is different, and there is never a Google article on how to open YOUR business, this is my advice to those who might be interested in going out on their own. DO IT! You'll never regret the moment you unlock your doors for the first time and realize you control your own fate. You'll learn that there is a love/hate relationship associated with your business. There will be certain times during the start-up phase of your business that there will be no free time or money to do the things you normally would have done in the past. However, there will be other times, typically after the start-up years, that your business will provide you freedoms that you never thought possible with any standard 8-5 job. The short-term sacrifice is certainly worth the long-term gain.

***

Brandon is the Owner & Manager of River Paws Pet Resort in Downtown Montgomery, Alabama. River Paws caters to those seeking upscale pet care services including dog daycare, pet boarding, training, and grooming services.

Before making his dream a reality Brandon attended Troy University where he studied Biology and worked at Taylor Crossing Animal Hospital. It was there that his love for animals and passion to be an entrepreneur took shape. After graduating from Troy, Brandon worked for his fraternity, Alpha Tau Omega, as a Leadership Consultant. For two years he traveled the country meeting leaders on campuses across the nation, all while preparing to start his own business.

The Personal Assistant - To Miss Universe

As an undergrad at the University of Nevada, Las Vegas (UNLV) studying Meetings & Events, I had the opportunity to work dozens of unique projects. In fact, we had to work over 1,000 hours in the field in order to graduate.

Many of these jobs were boring. I can't tell you how many times I was a human directional. Meaning, I'd stand in a hallway and use my best Flight Attendant impersonation skills to let convention attendees know where they needed to go. One time we had to help set up over 500 computers. I was behind the guy plugging in the power cords; I was on keyboards.

I got into arguments often. Not screaming in your

face arguments, nor even arguments where I was rude. I would just get guests who couldn't understand how deserts work. This conversation played out several times:

Guest: "How far is the Mojave Desert?"

Me: "we're in the desert right now."

Guest: "No, I mean like the desert desert."

Me: (confusedly) "I'm sorry ma'am, I'm not sure what you mean. We are in the desert right now."

Guest: "No we're not! We're on the Las Vegas Strip! Where is the desert?"

You can see how much fun that was...

Anyway, let's get to why you're here. The time I was the personal assistant to Miss Universe. It was the 10th Annual Latin Grammy Awards® at Mandalay Bay and they needed golf cart drivers. About 30 of us. I figured, $12 an hour, listen to Alicia Keys perform for free and a chance to meet a couple celebrities was a pretty great way to spend the evening.

I went to training and nothing special was happening. Our job was to take VIPs to and from various parts of the resort on golf carts, so they wouldn't have to walk.

Miss Universe was arriving and she needed a ride and an assistant for a while. They immediately asked me.

"She's from Venezuela, do you speak Spanish?"

"No."

"You'll do fine."

Moments later I met Stefanía Fernández. She was confident, beautiful, poised and so friendly. We chatted a bit and I answered all of her questions about Vegas, life in college and so on.

For those of you who aren't familiar, all of the major resorts in Las Vegas have secret passages, entrances, and exits for celebrities, royalty, and VIPs. There are varying levels to each of these. Some are less common routes, they're not secret per se, but they're relatively quiet most of the time.

I distinctly remember taking Stefania to one of these less traveled, yet not secret entrances into the resort. She had the most intense look of fear in her eyes as she simply said to me, "my fans."

I looked at her, perplexed. "Your fans?" I asked.

"They'll swarm on me. We need a more secret entrance."

I smiled and assured her we could take a more secret route, but that there would be a brief moment in which we'd have to walk through a portion of the casino. She hesitantly agreed.

I remember rolling my eyes (internally of course) and thinking, "who would recognize Miss Universe without an introduction? She is really full of herself."

I took her to the secret entrance and we got out of the golf cart. I looked ahead and reported back to her that the casino wasn't very busy. We should be good to go.

The instant she entered, the swarm came. People came out of the woodwork. I couldn't believe what was happening. Hundreds of people started running, full speed and screaming "Stefanía! Stefanía! Stefanía! We love you! Take a picture with us!" They kept coming. They kept screaming. We kept moving.

Let me tell you, I have never been more impressed with someone handling such a change in pace in my life. She kept walking, still as poised as ever, greeted her fans as she progressed through and I walked by her side like a bodyguard helping to keep people back.

When we were through, it was time for me to pass her off to her next handler. She looked at me. I'll never forget that look. Without a word she said, "I told you!" It wasn't a condescending "told ya so" moment, it was more of a "I warned you, you should've believed me" look. She thanked me, gave me a hug, we said our pleasantries, and I was off to my next assignment.

I learned a lot that night. I learned about some of the history and culture of Venezuela. I learned that Miss Universe was more than a pretty face. She was an accomplished, educated and determined woman who was passionate about many things, including the eradication of HIV/AIDS.

I learned about leadership and myself, too. I had a pretty big wakeup call that night, and I am so grateful that I did.

Just because you do not find interest in something, does not mean that others don't. I thought nothing of the Miss Universe pageant and assumed that was a worldwide held belief. I was sorely mistaken.

Stereotypes are not facts. Up until that fateful night I had only seen the worst side of pageants. The viral YouTube videos of contestants falling or answering questions poorly built my sole frame of reference. I learned that it's important to create your own opinions rather than allow the media or others to form them for you.

Lastly, I learned that you can teach others they're ignorant without being cruel, condescending, nor malicious. You can have poise and grace and still change the world.

***

Jordan has spoken on nearly 100 college campuses and started doing so since he was an undergraduate in college. Points of pride include being selected as the undergraduate commencement speaker for his class and keynoting a campus wide anti-hazing symposium. Since then he has worked for his fraternity, Alpha Tau Omega, and has overseen several signature programs. Jordan organized the sesquicentennial (that's 150!) celebration for the fraternity and wrote True Merit Character, the ground breaking membership education program used by all chapters in the country.

As the CEO of Andrew Reid Consultancy (ARC), Jordan oversees every aspect of the company. Rooted in values and focused on providing cutting edge programming, ARC works tirelessly to make a positive impact in the community.

Jordan has a knack for solving complex problems and developing innovative solutions. He has consulted and presented to various sized groups from one-on -one conversations to audiences as large as 20,000. Jordan is an accomplished speaker, author, and change agent.

The Nerd

Leadership is something that I never wanted to do, but always found myself pushed into. The thing is...I'm an introvert. Not even just an introvert, almost a misanthrope. I prefer numbers and data to people. I'm a nerd. "I hate people" is something that friends, family, and coworkers hear from me repeatedly. In my mind, people are irrational, and illogical, and messy—not like numbers and spreadsheets. Numbers and spreadsheets behave exactly the way you want them to. Which is what leads me to the interesting position of having been in leadership roles on and off for the past fifteen years of the nineteen years that I've been in the workplace.

My first leadership role came when I worked in Japan. I was about 22 years old and had never managed anyone before, other than an ill-fated stint as Assistant

Manager at a retail cookie store for about three weeks before my hatred of customers (customers = really hungry, extra irrational people) led me fleeing from the mall, vowing to never return. For some ridiculous reason, I was put in charge of a school of about 25. I was terrified and annoyed. I had come there to teach English for a couple of years, earn a paycheck, travel a little bit, and head home. I had no idea how to manage people.

I set out trying to learn how to manage. I was going to be fantastic because I was going to be everyone's friend. Because after all, isn't that the kind of boss that people really like? Unfortunately, I learned that strategy doesn't really work. First, if you're everyone's friend, you don't actually work at helping them identify their strengths and challenges, you don't actually make the tough decisions, so they don't respect you as a leader. And second, some people are just...well...not very good at their jobs, and they may take advantage of you if you're just trying to be their friend. I can't say that I excelled at leadership in that job in Japan, but I certainly learned what not to do.

My next experience was managing a small team of professionals at a state agency. They were diverse in age and experience. Again, I had to fight against my nature of just wanting to go into my office, open some spreadsheets, and close the door. The staff eyed me with skepticism, especially when I decided that this time I was going to come in completely hiding my terror at the fact that...I actually had no idea what I was doing. I knew nothing about the program areas I was going to be overseeing. So I walked in on day one, large and in charge, telling them exactly what they had been doing wrong and how I was going to change it. Wrong again. I discovered very, very quickly how soon this strategy backfired, as they began calling me out on what I didn't know.

Then I tried something novel. I thought, OK...if I'm looking at data, or trying to find the right statistical methodology to apply to a research project, what do I do if it's not working out the way I think it should? I dig into it. So I thought, ugh, people are gross, but let me try to figure out who they are. I'll take some time to figure out what they're doing, from their perspectives, and I won't come in acting like the expert, because I'm not. (I can also figure out what they like and don't like, and how my nerd skills can help them.)

I must have been onto something because it started to work. One of them really hated being micromanaged. She loved coming up with the ideas (but she needed help implementing them), and she really, really wanted respect for her age and the number of years she'd been doing the work. Another one CRAVED micromanagement. She wanted assurance that any idea she had was "right", or at least that it was the right way to go. The super young one really just wanted a mentor. And so on. I also discovered that one of them was really into figuring out how to measure her program's effectiveness. Sweet! I had found an outlet for my nerdiness. We worked together to create an accountability system, bringing in some of the program managers from outside to help us design it so that we'd have buy in from the external programs. We piloted the implementation, and I taught her how to run the numbers so that we could see which programs were effective and which needed intervention. She was so excited about it, and she grew so much confidence in being able to do it (this was the micromanagement craver) that she started to take initiative in other areas. She also acted as a champion for the others on the team to get them to see the value of implementing program effectiveness measures. We all came together as a team and ended up running programs that were recognized on a state and national level for our implementation and outcome measures.

After that, I found myself heading up an even larger, even more ragtag, band of Information Technology geeks. Now, if I thought I was an introvert, I apparently didn't know introverts. These IT guys and gals were a different breed of introvert. Again I was in over my head. While I knew data, I knew nothing about data systems, data warehousing, and other words that had no meaning to me. Again they regarded me with suspicion. What did I know about programming? What did I know about star schemas? Kirk or Picard??? It was overwhelming. As I struggled to figure out the content areas (and it's totally Kirk), I learned what I think might be the key to leadership success. Although all introverts, each of these IT geeks again had their own personalities, their own working styles, their own strengths, and their own weaknesses. So, like I had done with my previous staff (almost by accident), I met them where they were. The extreme, extreme introvert who could barely make eye contact with me? We spent our weekly meetings strictly talking about projects. We created clear project timelines together, and when he had to extend a deadline, I had his back on explaining the need for the deadline extension to my supervisor. The gal who really wanted to move into a leadership role but had no idea how to get past her difficulty talking to people? We worked on topics that she felt comfortable with, and then worked out ways to have her present to coworkers, first in very limited situations, and then to a larger group of coworkers, and then to an external audience where, despite being very nervous, she was great. Some people needed and wanted more guidance than others. Some people needed fires lit under them. Some people needed specific timelines, and others hated them. I came to appreciate the value—and this sounds weird—of treating people differently, depending on where they are. After thinking about it from a nerd perspective, this started to make a lot of sense. After all, you can't apply the same research methodology to all types of studies. If you try to apply the same outcomes analysis to all types of programs, it won't work. You have to tailor your methods. I guess it's the same with people.

Now I'm working in a large organization and managing, yet again, a variety of crazy people. They all have different styles, they all have different interests, and they all have different needs. Yet, we all try to meet each other where we are. We are working on trying to recognize strengths, and build upon those strengths, as opposed to focusing on weaknesses. I've determined that (because I love metaphors), in any given area, a person varies between a paper plate and a goblet. You can't pour coffee on a paper plate, and you can't turn a paper plate into a goblet. What you can do is turn a Dixie cup into an acrylic cup, into a glass, into a goblet. What I mean is, if you help someone understand where they either excel or could excel, you can help them turn into a goblet. But if you keep focusing on pouring coffee on a paper plate, it will dissolve (and fail, and likely leave the organization).

So after all of this, I've come to realize that people are perhaps not all that different from data and numbers. You can't get the kind of outcomes that you want if you are not applying the right kind of data and metrics. In much the same way, you can't get outcomes from people if you are not realizing who they are, where they are strong, and where they can contribute. Ultimately, this nerdy misanthrope has realized that while I still hate people, I actually love persons. And leading means understanding individuality within the group – a group is never monolithic!

***

Molly Chamberlin, Ph.D. is Executive Vice President at Thomas P. Miller and Associates, an international consulting firm in Indianapolis, Indiana. Dr. Chamberlin has an extensive background in evaluation, research, and policy, especially in the areas of K-12 and higher education. In her current role, she is responsible for overseeing a team of consultants who provide support for state and municipal government entities, institutions of higher education, non-profit organizations, workforce and economic development organizations, and private businesses in the areas of research, evaluation, and workforce and economic development.

She has worked with research, data analysis, and program evaluation in a variety of capacities, including federal and state programs and for-profit and non-profit organizations. Molly holds a Ph.D. in Educational Psychology from Indiana University, Bloomington, and a B.A. in Liberal Arts from Middlebury College, Middlebury, Vermont.

Molly currently lives in Indianapolis with her new husband, Nick, and their cat, Maggie.

The Marine

I've been an officer of Marines since March 26, 2016, and a student at one of the most intensive leadership schools in the world (Officer Candidates School) for 69 days prior. I've never been in combat, and I've yet to hold my first command, but the United States Marine Corps has invested thousands of hours training me to lead veteran Marines who have.

The Marine Corps sends all of its newly commissioned officers to a six-month long basic officer course known as "The Basic School" (TBS), a program unlike any other in the United States military. Here, we are taught to make a "70-percent decision," or to decide and act quickly with just 30-percent of the facts.

During a training exercise in Quantico, VA in July 2016, I was acting platoon commander of a provisional infantry platoon, made up of 46 second lieutenants. The platoon had been conducting continuous operations for four days in the oppressive summer heat and the human factors of training were beginning to take their toll on the Marines.

We were tasked with locating and destroying an "enemy" platoon, who were fortified and protected in deep fighting positions. We had an estimate of where they were, what kind of equipment they had, and what they were doing to stop us; however, nothing was certain. It was my job to figure it out and provide the subordinate leaders in my charge the tools necessary to accomplish our mission.

The toolbox I provided them with all began with an order, or a well-developed and thought out plan. I provided as many specific details as possible while still leaving room for flexibility and initiative from my subordinate leaders. Next, I conducted a leader's reconnaissance of the enemy, where I actively sought answers to our earlier estimations and re-briefed my subordinate leaders on the newest information available. Once this was done, it was time to allow my subordinates to viciously carry out the plan against the enemy.

As we began executing the mission, our supervisors introduced external chaos and friction to me and my Marines. With blank ammunition, pyrotechnics, and a living enemy in front of us, the Captains began their frenzy of chaos. The Captain evaluating me began constantly asking what I was going to do, just as my Marines were asking how I wanted them to act. "Helmet

Fire," a term used to describe a leader becoming overwhelmed with his thoughts and incapable of making a timely decision, was beginning to set in on me. At this moment, the chaos settled and what needed to be done became incredibly clear. I had developed a plan, confirmed my estimate of the enemy, and given my Marines as many tools as I could. All we had to do was execute it and look past the external friction.

When I realized this, all that was left for me to do was coordinate between my units and my boss, remaining flexible and allowing decentralized leadership to run its course.

Adaptability has long been the Marine way to overcome friction. According to Marine Corps Warfighting Publication 6-11, Leading Marines, "The ability to adapt enables Marines to be comfortable within an environment dominated by friction. Experience, common sense, and the critical application of judgement all help Marine leaders persevere." I believe this ability to adapt in chaos comes from our training and our shared belief in the end state of our mission. With this, the leaders appointed over us give us the freedom to decide and act independently at our level of execution.

The Marine Corps trains us to work at an incredible level of decentralized leadership. This is the process of giving our subordinates enough "tools" and intent to make their own decisions on how to execute. Our Marines are trained to a standard, over and over again until they can't get it wrong, then they execute violently. The concept of decentralized leadership is applied over and over again, giving small unit leaders the ability to adapt as necessary, guided by their commander's intent and desired result.

As officers, we are instilled with five horizontal themes during our training that empower us to lead through adversity:

1. Be a man or woman of exemplary character

2. Be devoted to leading Marines 24/7

3. Be able to decide, communicate, and act in the fog of war

4. Be a Warfighter who embraces the Corps' warrior ethos

5. Be mentally strong and physically tough

If understood, these horizontal themes can be applied to any situation and turn an average leader into an exceptional one.

The most important thing for a leader, especially a leader of Marines, is to keep a balance between mission accomplishment and the welfare of your Marines. As leaders, our decisions on the battlefield are permanent; our Marines live and die by them, as the currency we deal with is human lives. This is not the case for most people, especially those outside of the military, but the lessons here remain true.

What I learned during my evolution as a platoon commander was more valuable than any lessons a book or lecture could provide. I saw firsthand that leadership, and people willingly following you, comes from the five themes above. If you're a genuine person and willing to put those in your charge before yourself, they will execute anything for you: but you must do it always, with no exceptions. You must be able to take whatever information you have, make a decision, and communicate it to everyone – down to the absolute lowest level. It is imperative that you embrace your organization's mission and live it to the fullest extent. Finally, as the leader, you are bound by an obligation to those you are entrusted to lead them through their mission from the front, wholeheartedly.

***

Creighton is a native of the great state of Tennessee. After living in both Nashville and Memphis, he has an ear for great music and an acute taste for barbeque. He is a graduate of the University of Missouri, where he majored in Radio/TV Journalism and Political Science and was a proud member of the Alpha Tau Omega Fraternity. After graduating from college, Creighton was a congressional intern in Washington D.C. before being selected as an Officer Candidate in the United States Marine Corps. Upon Commissioning in March of 2016, he was designated as a Logistics Officer. As of August 2017, Creighton has the honor and privilege of serving more than 80 Marines as the Platoon Commander for Motor Transport Platoon, Service Company, 7th Communication Battalion in Okinawa, Japan.

The International Educator

When thinking about my future career choices in college, moving to another country to teach English had never crossed my mind. The conventional wisdom is that you are supposed to graduate, find a job near where you live, move up in a great company, and stay there for as long as you can. Well, I decided to go an unconventional route and move to Indianapolis for two years after college to become a traveling consultant. I enjoyed being out of my comfort zone, so I decided to take it to another extreme in July of 2015. I was hired to become an international educator in Urumqi, Xinjiang, China.

I landed in the Urumqi airport on the night of July 15th, 2015. I was in a place where I didn't know the language, food, customs, geography, etc. Soon, though, I became more comfortable with living in China but I would face my biggest task yet - teaching English as a foreign language. The Director of Studies for the school approached me after my first week to let me know that I would be teaching my first class the next day. I freaked out, I had nothing prepared and I was not sure how the students would receive me.

I stayed up all night thinking about what to do with my class. I knew that they were 8-9 year olds and they had a reputation for fighting in class, but this was early. Come to find out, the previous teacher wanted to give them away to the new teacher (me). Now I was anxious; I thought the students wouldn't understand me, I did not know how to handle wild children and, most importantly, I had never taught before. I knew I was pretty good at my old job (consulting) but I had no idea if that would translate into being a good teacher.

The morning came and I knew, that ready or not, I would teach my first class TODAY. I got into work a bit earlier than I had to so that I could make last minute preparations. I planned what I thought to be an hour class plus a bit extra just in case the students were faster than I had anticipated. I walked into class and it immediately hit me that I had to be in control. There were three students fighting and a little girl frantically telling me what they were fighting about - in Chinese; Luckily, I broke up the fight by yelling, "That's enough!" I then remembered that these were 8-9 year old Chinese kids who didn't understand obscure English phrases. So I yelled, "Be quiet and sit down!" Much more effective!

As the class went along, I became frustrated with a

few students who didn't seem to understand what I was asking. I thought I was giving pretty clear instructions to them but they looked at me like I was speaking a different language (oh yeah, I was!). It kicked in that they just couldn't understand a few words I was using. So I sat down with the students and tried to use more body language and simple words they knew to explain what I was expecting them to do. Sure enough, they then understood and did their work perfectly.

The end of the class finally came an hour later and I was both relieved and proud. Everything didn't go according to plan but that was a good thing. I was able to learn from my mistakes and make notes on how to improve for next time. I learned three big lessons from my first class: I would need an amount of patience I didn't think I had; I should always have a back up plan; and I should utilize past experiences.

As an international educator, the biggest obstacle in teaching is always the language barrier. It is a unique situation where the students and teacher literally speak two different languages. After my first class, I knew that I would have to become much more patient than I had ever been. I did become frustrated with the few students who didn't seem to understand the work that I was giving them, but after my frustration was gone, I was able to sit down and try to think of a simpler way to explain what they needed to do. It paid off. The students felt good about being able to do their work and I felt accomplished as an educator. Over the past year, my patience has improved. I've even become used to my students not being able to understand the first, second or even third time I explain what I need them to do.

After that first class, I also learned that I should always over prepare. Like I said earlier, I tried to over prepare for the one-hour class. I only had time to teach about half of what I had planned because I did not take into account the extra time needed to explain difficult instructions that the students may not understand. But, I also noticed that I had to ditch some of my plans because the students just couldn't understand. So I knew I would always need a backup plan just in case. It is better to be over prepared than under prepared.

Additionally, during that first class, I did not take advantage of past experiences enough. When my class was going crazy, it brought flashbacks of my time as a fraternity president trying to run a meeting or as a consultant trying to get a college student's attention. I had plenty of presentation experience from my past that I just hadn't thought about using until the time came. Using my past experience to help with my new obstacles turned out to be the best way to control classrooms. I have used plenty of games and icebreakers from previous presentations to get my class ready or calm them down.

My biggest takeaway from not only my first class but as an international educator is that we cannot forget how to communicate face to face. In this digital era, it is easy to just send an email or text and go on with your day. But what about when you are in front of a group of people who cannot understand what you are trying to say? Or in my case, they literally can't understand. You need to think of different and better ways to convey your message incorporating body language, eye contact and hand motions so that an audience or class can understand. I also realized that every new experience leaves me with a new arsenal of abilities that I can utilize later in my life and career. Never discount how your past experience helps in future situations.

My first class was exactly a year ago last week. Today, I taught them for the last time as I am moving to a new city in China to teach. I value all of the lessons that I have learned that I never would have had without this experience.

***

My name is Ryne Alexander. I am 26 years old and I am from the great city of Nolensville, Tennessee which is right outside Nashville. I graduated from Middle Tennessee State University with a Bachelor's Degree in Organizational Communication. After living in the same state for all of my life, I was itching to see something new. This led me to reject my entrance into Graduate School and take a consulting position with Alpha Tau Omega National Fraternity in Indianapolis, Indiana. This consulting position allowed me to visit 30 different college campuses in ten different states. This is when I knew that I just had not seen enough of the world around me. That led me to applying for and accepting a teaching position in Urumqi, Xinjiang, China with English First. After a year in this city, I moved to Hangzhou, Zhejiang, China to work for the same company. I am still in Hangzou today and love living and teaching abroad. Outside of work, I am interested in physical fitness, specifically running. I am training for my first marathon, which I will compete in in November of this year.

The Captain

On the seas we have a motto that dictates all facets of our operations: Modify, Adapt, Overcome. We repeat it constantly, and it has proven to be invaluable in my growth as a Captain and a leader. Modifications, Adaptions and Overcoming obstacles can take many forms. Sometimes as a Captain you need to act as the deckhand for a day, on other days you're piloting your vessel.

What started as a beautiful windy day, quickly turned into a lesson of leadership for me. I was the Chief Engineer on our 150ft Columbia Gorge Sternwheeler (looks like a large ferry boat with the giant wheel on the back spinning) as we sailed through the Columbia River.

On any of our typical landmark cruises we depart from our dock in Cascade Locks and head downriver to the Bonneville Dam. From there we venture to Beacon Rock, Multnomah Falls and Cape Horn. If you're not familiar with these areas, you should Google them, they're both historic and gorgeous!

Things were going well and the acting Captain maneuvered the vessel and brought our bow (front) right up to our forward dolphin (similar to a dock but not connected to land). I took the bow line that is fixed to the dolphin and secured it to the cleat onboard our vessel. As the Captain continued to maneuver astern (backwards) the dolphin began to break. All of the wood pilings began to crumble and fall towards our ship. They hit the water and splashed as the structure quickly began to collapse.

Within the blink of an eye I mulled my options and took action, knowing that with 50 souls onboard the first decisions needed to be the right one. I hastily undid my previous cleating and separated us from the now demolished dolphin.

I knew from earlier interactions that day that my deckhand wasn't feeling well. Where I would normally find myself with assistance, I now found myself alone. My eyes sought the Captain's Lookout.

"All gone!" I yelled only once, but clearly to ensure she was aware of the situation without inciting fear into our passengers.

The Lookout then explained to our Captain what happened and they began discussing possible plans of action moving forward.

As is the case anytime you're on the water, the wind had a big impact in moving our vessel and we as pilots are trained to use that to our advantage. We also knew we were a man down and could not rely on help from our deckhand.

Together, we decided our best option would be to dock the vessel by placing our midship (middle part of the boat) onto another nearby dolphin. We would then secure those lines and use our boarding ramp to de board from our bow.

The biggest challenge we faced was the lineup of the ramp to our bow gate. Once we had a few lines secure we were less than an inch away from a perfect line up. We were able to get one side of the ramp down and then made it ready for safe passage so we de boarded our passengers.

During this process (as if there wasn't enough going on) I had open communication with our Cruise Manager to help keep our passengers safe and informed.

Once we had all of our passengers safely off the vessel we were able to rig mooring lines about 50ft to shore. Our bow line was secured to a very large tree and our stern line was secured to a concrete block on shore. These makeshift lines were much longer, heavier and more difficult to handle but we continued to dock our vessel this way for the rest of the season. It made docking more difficult but we managed to finish out the season with zero incidents. Thankfully a new steel dolphin was installed in early spring when divers were able to complete the job safely.

***

Jessica attended Our Lady of Mercy High School in Rochester, New York. While there, she lettered in Soccer, Lacrosse, and Basketball. It was also during her High School tenure that she was introduced to her current passion and profession: sailing.

What started as a casual summer job, chartering Catamaran cruises on Lake Ontario, became, in time, so much more. For multiple summers Jessica worked on the ship, earning her stripes and advancing from crewmember to First Mate and eventually earned her Mariner's Captain license.

She walked away from being a Captain, thinking it wasn't a practical future and decided to go to college. Jessica was recruited to play lacrosse and studied Elementary Education.

It wasn't long before the call of the ocean became too strong to ignore. Jessica returned to her roots and has worked on dozens of vessels. Currently, she is a Captain for Portland Spirit Cruises in Downtown Portland, Oregon. In her free time, she enjoys playing sports, traveling and spending time with the greatest dog ever, Lola Mimosa (as pictured).

The Pilot

My dad always said, "Don't pick a career you hate or you'll be miserable every day you wake up" which is true to an extent. I took that to heart when I was young, and I still look back on it now. I grew up seeing him miserable throughout his days, waking up early and working later and later without much happiness for what he wanted to do outside of work. It was a constant struggle of fatigue and stress. Time seemed to just fly away and things to do never ended.

I never really set out on finding the "perfect" career, it just fell into place. I liked flying on airlines when I was young, so when I had the opportunity to take a lesson, I did. And a short time later I found myself sitting in a cockpit, by myself, for the first time. I had found something I loved and it was now time to see how much I learned and remembered. My instructor hopped out and said, "Go do 3, good luck!" He shut the door behind him and I was on my own for about the next 30 minutes. Nervous, sweating, and excited all at the same time, I was now in charge and had to make all the decisions myself. The first three landings by yourself are never the best, but I had the opportunity to experience something that few have. By the end of it, I was hooked. I didn't think of the challenges that came next; I just knew I found what I wanted to do.

I gained a little bit of confidence the day I soloed. I switched roles. I became the leader, the only leader, but nevertheless the leader. I did not realize this roll of following and leading would happen over and over to get me where I am today. The goal was clear, but the path was not. I had to take the next four years to continue to learn and be a follower before I could prove that I could be a leader in the airplane teaching students. As I worked through all of my ratings I remember doing most everything exactly as my instructor had explained. I was nervous and new to each new item I had to learn. This is how I "played it safe." I did things this way to learn and grow, but as I gained more knowledge I still needed to be receptive to other ideas or other ways to do things. I developed comfort by experiencing new ways of doing something and respecting others' ideas.

The first time I was truly in a leadership role was like the first time I had soloed an airplane, but this time it was my student. I was still sweaty, nervous, and excited all at once. He had been a great student but if I wasn't confident, if I wasn't a good teacher, if I wasn't a good leader, it could have been a different result at the end of the day. Sitting in the control tower knowing I was responsible for everything that the student did on his own was an empowering yet humbling experience. At this point in time I really hoped my feeling of, “he's ready” was correct. With three landings, It turned out to be a successful day for him as it has been for me years before. He had experienced his first time being a leader in the cockpit. His journey had just begun and mine had more to go through.

I still had learning to go through and therefore still needed to be able to be a follower. I needed to be able to switch roles as I learned how to teach more advanced students and in more advanced airplanes. I needed to learn how to take advice and give advice in the same day and in some cases, with the same student. Even though a student may not have been at my skill level and knowledge level, everyone did things slightly different. This is when I really learned to listen to ideas and suggestions they brought up as they tried to master a new goal. Actually listening to the students opinions and trying out different methods to achieve a task, made me better as an instructor. In turn, I could now be a better teacher and leader in the airplane. By this point, it was not just about airplanes; it was about developing a skill of switching roles from one to another to grow as a leader in my field.

The biggest challenge was when I moved from teaching to actually flying passengers. By this time I thought I knew a lot and I thought I was good at what I did. And in some respects, I was. But, as I sit as a first officer I still need to grow my skills and abilities as a follower as I now have a more experienced captain to my left. I had to be humble from my experiences and learn from what the captain could teach me. As I continue through my journey of the airlines, this role switching between a leader and a follower will never end. I'll make my journey to the captain's role and head into different places and eventually into bigger and more advanced aircrafts.

The message I bring is simple. To be a successful leader you must be a good follower. When you are in a leadership role you still need to be humble and learn from those around you, regardless of who they are or what their job is. Leadership is learned and enhanced by experiences that we all live through each and every day. Without humility and an open mind you stop being teachable and you stop growing as a leader in your respective field.

***

Nick is a graduate of the world renowned Department of Aviation at the John D. Odegard School of Aerospace Sciences at the University of North Dakota. Nick is currently an airline transport pilot for Hyannis Air Service, Inc. Outside of aviation and traveling he is dedicated to becoming a successful entrepreneur through helping others grow and develop as a leader in their respective fields.

The Sailor

From the day I sat on the pier watching USS Lake Champlain approaching for the first time, to the day that I looked upon her as I was walking away for the last time, I knew my life had changed forever. More specifically, it was a man named Chief Petty Officer Santos who had turned me from a person who was counting down the days until I left, into a sailor who strived to be better at everything we did, and always continue to learn.

The beginning of my Navy career would start off fairly easy, but rougher waters were waiting ahead. In June 2008 I reported to a shore command called Aviation Support Detachment in Ventura County, California. Shore duty is known navy-wide as the place where sailors get some R&R after arduous duty at sea: often seen as an incentive for sailors to stay in the Navy. This duty was easy; there was nothing hard or arduous about it. Being that it was my first command, I was under the impression that Navy life was going to be easy, despite what my counterparts were telling me. I thought, "20 years? Who wouldn't or couldn't do this?" I was wrong; I just didn't know it yet.

Sea duty had finally arrived for me, and with it, all the growing pains I was about to endure. I reported to USS Lake Champlain in August of 2010, and my first year onboard was absolutely hell. A month after I checked onboard, we deployed for 7 months. In the span of that deployment I quickly learned what actual Navy life was about: long days, constant stress, time away from my wife and friends, repetitive work, drills every day, etc. Halfway through the deployment I was already in the mode of "I hate this job," "I'm getting out," "This is stupid," and so forth. To add to all of this, a new Senior Chief had reported onboard and everyone quickly realized, this Senior Chief was here to get promoted, and he was going to do so off the backs of his people.

This was the first lesson I learned in leadership: what not to do when I become a leader someday. After 6 months of what I can only describe as a "reign of terror" under this Senior Chief our division's morale was at an all-time low. People just didn't care anymore; it wasn't uncommon to hear people say: "why do jobs well anyways? Senior is just going to tell us it isn't right, or he could do it better." We were just getting through the motions, work wasn't being done properly, and we were literally hiding paperwork that was supposed to be filed, just so we could get out of there and avoid any extra time with Senior Chief.

It was at this time that Logistics Specialist First Class Ireno Santos reported onboard (or LS1 for short.) He would be promoted to Chief Petty Officer (or LSC) a week later. First impressions from everyone in the division were that he could be even worse than Senior Chief. He came in demanding respect, he wanted things done the right way, liberty (Navy term for being off duty) waited until the job not only was done, but done correctly. In my current mindset of just getting by at the bare minimum, I didn't care for him at first, and I knew he didn't care for me either. It was obvious to him I was lazy and unreliable; because of this, he was even harder on me.

Fast forward 6 months, things were getting better. I think to this day, it's because the division realized that Chief Santos wasn't as bad as we all originally thought. Yes, he demanded excellence, but it was also blatantly obvious that he cared about his people. To the Senior Chief, we were expendable resources in his quest to promote to Master Chief. With Chief Santos, we were a team that needed to get a job done, and he was not only going to make sure we finished the job, but that he was going to teach us how to get the job done. Senior Chief Stalin (not his actual name for the record) finally transferred off the ship to another command. This meant that Chief Santos was finally going to oversee the division.

Now at this point I was beginning to see a new light; I could feel my motivation skyrocketing. I'll never forget in his first speech to the division he stated; "Guys I'm the division Chief now, and I'm going to tell you right now things are going to be different." We all smiled because we knew this could only mean for the better. His style of leading was hard to grasp at first; he was never shy to call someone out if they messed up, even in front of everyone else in most cases. But the way he did it was what motivated me (and I'm sure everyone else.) He used humor, he would crack jokes. I used to take deep breaths when he would get on my case, and he'd say things like, "Voll do you have asthma? You're always breathing hard man, what's going on man? You need to go to medical?" I couldn't help but laugh at this. It was then I realized the most important lesson of my life. You can demand excellence from people, but can do it in a way that was informal, sometimes unprofessional, and ultimately: personal.

Nobody was safe from the wrath of his jokes, including him. Other people would complain that they never saw their wives, he would respond; "Hey man, your wife didn't come in your sea bag." This would almost always infuriate most people, but to us, this level of "talking smack" was beginning to become our rallying cry. Better yet, when we did catch him messing up, (although rare) we could then give him a taste of his own medicine and he would own it, or at the very least joke that it was only one out of every 100 WE made. His style not only made us all better, but it made the division come together and form a bond unlike anything I've ever known or experienced.

Today I have since moved on from the ship and we all have gone our own separate ways. I myself have held a couple of different leadership roles since those days. I have employed a lot of his style mixed with my own. I have seen mostly positive results from this and I truly believe it is the best way to lead. Most of the "old crew" still stays in touch to this day despite being separated by thousands of miles. I plan to separate from the Navy in the next year, but I already plan to bring the leadership principles I learned from him to the civilian sector. Things I never thought I could do, I am now doing. Because whenever I get the urge to quit, give up, or take the lazy route, I can almost hear Chief Santos in the back of my mind saying, "Come on man, what's the status? Do you have asthma today?"

***

Ryan Voll is currently an enlisted U.S. Navy Sailor who has been on active duty since 2008 as a Navy Logistics Specialist. He has served in several leadership roles in his time in the Navy, most of which required high degrees of adaptability due to the high turnover rate of personnel. He has earned three Navy achievement medals for outstanding performance and leadership at three different Navy organizations around the world. He currently plans to transition from the Navy to the civilian workplace where he wants to finish his Business degree and seek employment as a government contracting officer. Ryan lives in Naples, Italy with his wife, Heather.

The Realtor

In fairness, this is not an ordinary leadership story, it's a sort of an antihero version. I'd been in the real estate business for a year or so when I learned an invaluable leadership lesson. Sometimes seeing what not to do can be just as valuable as learning what to do, I was surprised to discover. Prior to getting my real estate license, I had been a stay-at-home mom for almost fifteen years and felt a certain amount of trepidation about entering the business world after functioning for such a long time as the quintessential soccer mom. I was determined to succeed, but also intimidated by pretty much every facet of the job.

The escrow in a real estate transaction is the period after an offer on a property is accepted until the closing, when the home 'sells' and officially changes hands to a new owner. About a year into the job, I met a client who was charming, tall and good looking with dark hair and a teenage son who was a sweet, gangly version of himself. His wife was tidy and self-contained. Kevin told me over and over that all he wanted was 'a home for his family'. Both his wife and home-schooled son came to every home showing, though they generally didn't say much.

After some time, we found a home, got an offer accepted and were working through the escrow process, with some difficulty, as the seller was out-of-state and working through some legal issues pertaining to the property. A week or so away from closing, we received the HOA package, an item the seller must provide per state law, which included detailed financials and contains rules and regulations governing the homeowner's association along with other details. In the package, a notification was included noting minor litigation, something to do with exterior property walls. Kevin was furious about the litigation and decided to cancel the escrow, which was well within his rights. Still, I was confused. This type of litigation is generally minor, had nothing to do with the structure of the home and is usually resolved to the homeowner's satisfaction. He was getting the home at a fantastic price and it had pretty much everything on his wish list. Didn't he want a home for his family? Turned out, what he wanted was a great deal on his singular and definitive terms. I drew up a cancellation which refunded his earnest deposit.

Now, a real estate agent doesn't get paid until an escrow closes. I had spent countless hours showing property, writing and negotiating offers, communicating with the seller's attorney's office to move the escrow forward, arranging the home inspection, answering questions, and communicating with the title company. And I wasn't going to get a paycheck. While disappointing, it's the nature of the business and he had every right to cancel the escrow if something in the HOA package was not to his liking. I wanted what was best for Bruce and his family and volunteered to assist them in finding a rental, since they had decided not to look for another home.

When I showed up to open the door of the rental house, I could tell he was steaming. They looked through the house quickly, Kevin sneering at the poor paint job and when we stepped outside, he started in, his voice rising the longer he spoke. Soon after he began yelling at me in the driveway, his wife and son slunk back to the SUV. They quietly closed the doors, even though it must have been stifling in the summer sun. Clearly, this was not their first rodeo. As I stood there listening to him yell about the injustice done to him, the time he had spent and the couple hundred bucks he had paid for the home inspection, it came to me suddenly that his tirade had nothing whatsoever to do with me. I had done my job in every sense of the word. I had asked questions and listened at length as he and his wife discussed what they wanted in a home. I had researched and shown them dozens of homes that might have been a good fit. I had worked through a challenging negotiation involving an attorney's office, dealt with an inexperienced agent on the selling side, made sure all contingencies of the contract were satisfied and kept my good humor with a client who was difficult and demanding through-out (when Kevin didn't get the answer he wanted from me, he would sometimes call my broker to complain). It was as if he could force a positive outcome for himself with enough charm, bluster and sincere sounding bonhomie, which I imagine had worked for him many times in his life. When that didn't happen to his specification in this situation, he wanted someone to blame.

I learned two leadership lessons from this escrow – one: to listen to the words behind the words (more accurately, to pay attention to actions, regardless of the rhetoric) and two: to take accountability when it was mine to take and leave it when it was not mine.

Later, I took a class about cutting edge technology in the real estate business. Two things the instructor said stuck with me. One: an iPhone is like a reliable car, easy to navigate to get where you're going. An Android is like the space shuttle, it can do brilliant things but you've got to be committed to learning what all the buttons and switches are for, or it will sit, clunky and earthbound, nose pointed up with nowhere to go. I'll take the iPhone any day! But I digress. Two: he quoted an old Polish proverb, "Not my circus, not my monkeys." He drew a visual picture and spoke about being aware enough to see the difference.

Taking accountability when it's my circus is extremely important. A good leader knows when the monkeys running wild are her own, she acknowledges responsibility and takes immediate and definitive steps to correct the error as quickly as possible.

Besides the fact that 'trying' to corral someone else's monkeys is virtually impossible, it also sends the message the person isn't capable of handling their own problems, which is disempowering. I learned that I can be effective and efficient when I stay out of other peoples' mental business, and stay in my own. The ability to be clear, loving and present is a gift I give to my clients and myself.

I realized that's what had happened in the driveway of that house those many years ago. Kevin did his best to bully me into taking several 'monkeys', Frustration, Discontent and Outrage that things had not gone his way. I imagine it felt awful to be him in that moment, one monkey pulling his hair, the other sticking its finger up his nose, while the third hooted in his ear. I stood there attending to the rise and fall of his voice and didn't take a single monkey. I listened politely until he was done, all the while knowing his distress had nothing to do with me, wished him well and got in my car and drove away, feeling calm, peaceful and ready for my next real estate adventure!

***

Learning to read was like opening a magic door to worlds colored with a different set of paints than the ones used for the dusty streets of her small Arizona town. In first grade Lara wrote stories of her own and when she discovered in third grade that she could check out one book a day, instead of just once a week on the library visit with her class, she was overjoyed. She read on the bus riding home and if she missed the bus she read while she walked home. She developed the habit of reading while brushing her teeth, which is a tough habit to break. Every day she brought back the book she had read and checked out another. Weekends stretched long with only one book to get her through. Alas, grown-ups need money to buy toothbrushes, and since publishing jobs are lean on the ground in Las Vegas NV, she got her real estate license and these days she sells homes between books instead of going to school. This works out well because she loves people and thinks that buying a home is a life-changing experience and feels privileged her clients allow her to assist with this important job. She got her associates degree from the College of Southern Nevada (CSN) and when she's not showing homes or reading, she enjoys spending time with her friends, three amazing children and her fabulous husband.

The Super Bowl Coordinator

You've heard of it. In fact we all have heard of it. Just after the high of Christmas and New Year's celebrations, it is the next big event to come around. Whether you are a fan or not, the NFL Super Bowl is a highly anticipated affair each year. As the most watched sporting event in the nation, and one of the top five most watched sporting events in the world, approximately 112 million viewers tuned in to watch the league's Super Bowl 50 this year. Which, astonishingly, is actually not the highest recorded amount of viewers; that title belongs to the 2014 Super Bowl XLIX. This event is so massive that millions of dollars are spent in team apparel, TV commercial space, game day tickets, travel, and much more. Household name musicians are booked almost a half of a year in advance only to perform the national anthem or a handful of songs for roughly twelve minutes. Hosting cities typically spend insane amounts of money to prep, but also reap the financial benefits of accommodating approximately 78,000 people. But what and who does it take to put on something of this magnitude?

As a sports enthusiast: with a degree in sports management and a dedicated fan of the NFL, working for the Super Bowl, at any level, pretty much sums up to be a dream opportunity. Indianapolis had won the 2011 season bid and my city was to host Super Bowl XLVI on February 5, 2012.

My initial involvement was simple. A logistics and parking company that had been contracted by the Super Bowl, as well as other major entertainment events, was creating a call center located in Indianapolis, built of local individuals and managed by experienced employees. Two weeks, long hours, average pay, and your epitome of a valley of death of customer service and you have my first employment experience with the Super Bowl. Doesn't sound fancy, but it was outstanding to me and I quickly learned a couple of things:

1. There isn't one committee planning this event. There are committees times twenty, and each more than likely has its own subcommittee(s). Parking and logistics? You're looking at 5-7 employment teams alone.

2. These management committees are tight knit groups. All friends, all excited to be at the Super Bowl, all have worked previous Super Bowls and/or other major sporting events, and all have advanced within. The management teams weren't from Indianapolis. No, they traveled from all over the nation, either employed by the logistics company or started with a "bottom of the totem pole" position and was asked to come back next year at a higher level.

So I took this opportunity and I did my best to make the most of it. I made contacts and built up my network. I wanted to make an impression and I wanted to return for next year's event; and so I did. I got the email asking if I was interested in returning to the Super Bowl employment team at a new position and if I could move to New Orleans for a month. I don't want to be dramatic, but that email was almost as thrilling as being an eleven year old getting their acceptance letter to Hogwarts. And it felt that way for each year after.

Through this journey of Super Bowls, I was able to live in new places, continue to meet new people, and expand my knowledge of this event and all that goes into it. Let's return back to the half-time show. I'm confident you could ask a handful of people who the entertainers were for the past few Super Bowls and you'd get the immediate response "Beyoncé, Bruno Mars, Katy Perry. Oh! And Coldplay!" Side note: No surprise Coldplay would be last in a list considering they were supposed to be the headliners and ended up awkwardly shadowing Beyoncé and her squad of strong women commanding the field this last year. But to my point, it's easy to name these people. They are household names. Their names alone are brands and they are marketed for weeks leading up to the event date. But tell me – do you think Katy Perry built that lion she rode out on? Or Beyoncé was there with a headset to que the back-up dancers onto the field? Or how about Bruno Mars? Do you think he carefully planned out the blueprints of his stage and wired his mic? You get the point. I had the privilege of getting to know some of these people behind the scenes of these shows. Let me assure you, there is A LOT more that goes into a twelve minute show than you'd think. Their planning starts the day the artist is decided on, and each meeting is more crucial than the last one.

So what can you take from this? Leadership doesn't always necessarily mean you will be the "big man on campus." You can make the effort, take initiative, and strive to not be a seat filler. Small actions in small roles that help the overall team is leadership and can progress into new opportunities. Additionally, leadership isn't always glorious or rewarding. Your role may not be fancy, or you may not get the recognition you deserve. It takes a massive amount of people to come together to ensure an event of this size runs smoothly. Yet, the credit of them is hardly acknowledged to the general public. Every February you can name a celebrity musician and a list of NFL pro-athletes, but it isn't those people who provide a safe and successful affair. So when in a leadership role, understand if your team that supports you is succeeding, and your event, or service, or product is doing well, then you as a leader have created a path for that success.

***

Kristen has been helping companies re-brand and strategize for nearly a decade. Her Midwestern charm and authentic approach ensures that both clients and customers are excited about the final product. Kristen is a native of Indianapolis, the self-proclaimed biggest Colts fan in the world, and a true Hoosier at heart. She currently lives in sunny Phoenix where she oversees all logistics, branding and marketing for Andrew Reid Consultancy (ARC).

You'd be hard pressed to find someone with a more remarkable or impressive resume than Kristen. She was a Logistics Coordinator for 3 Super Bowls (XL VI - Indianapolis, XL VII - New Orleans, XL VIII - New York / New Jersey), served as the Director of Marketing for a camp during the 75th Sturgis Motorcycle Rally and was a Client Services Manager for one of the most successful management consulting firms in the US. Considered an expert in the industry, Kristen specializes in ensuring a brand's image and promise.

The Next Chapter

This chapter took, perhaps the longest to take shape. I thought about so many options... do we summarize what we've learned? Do we end with a famous quotation? Do we end the book?

After much consideration, one thing was crystal clear. There couldn't be an ending. After all, each letter from our authors gave us a glimpse into their life, shared compelling stories and taught us lessons.

I hope, that if nothing else, the lesson you've learned is that everyone has a story. This includes you!

The next chapter, won't be written by us. It'll be written by you. On the next few pages, you'll find space to add your letter so that when you re-read this book (or gift it!) you'll be able to reminisce in your personal letter too.

Your friend in leadership,

A. Jordan Fischette

YOUR PHOTO HERE

Made in the USA
Columbia, SC
26 October 2023